LETTERS

TO THE

HON. WILLIAM JAY,

BEING

A REPLY TO HIS "INQUIRY

INTO THE

AMERICAN COLONIZATION

AND

AMERICAN ANTI-SLAVERY SOCIETIES."

BY DAVID M. REESE, M. D.

OF NEW YORK

NEGRO UNIVERSITIES PRESS

NEW YORK

Originally published in 1835
by Leavitt, Lord & Co., New York

Reprinted from a copy in the collections
of the Brooklyn Public Library

Reprinted 1970 by
Negro Universities Press
A DIVISION OF GREENWOOD PRESS, INC.
NEW YORK

SBN 8371-2911-7

PRINTED IN UNITED STATES OF AMERICA

RECOMMENDATIONS.

*From the Rev. John Breckinridge, President of the Young Men's Co-
lonization Society of Pennsylvania.*

New-York, May 13, 1835.

I have examined with much interest and satisfaction, the proof
sheets of the chief parts (the whole being not quite complete) of Dr.
Reese's "Letters to the Hon. Wm. Jay," in reply to his late work
against the American Colonization Society.

Dr. Reese has largely merited the thanks of the American people,
for the prompt and satisfactory manner in which he has refuted and
exposed a work, which, upon a momentous and agitating question,
and under an imposing name, has said more *disingenuous, sophistical,*
and yet *dangerous* things, than I had supposed it possible to be uttered
in so small a compass, by so honest, so good, and so sensible a man.

JOHN BRECKINRIDGE.

From the Rev. Drs. Milnor, Brownlee, and De Witt.

Dear Sir,—Having been favoured with the opportunity of reading
the proof sheets of a large portion of your answer to the recent publication of the Hon. William Jay, assailing the principles and proceedings of the American Colonization Society, we beg leave to express
our approbation of the views which you have presented; and to add,
that, in our opinion, you have very successfully defended the Institution against the charges in the book referred to, exposed the mistakes
and errors of its worthy author, and presented arguments and facts,
as we conceive, abundantly sufficient to satisfy every impartial mind
of the preference which should be given to the practical operations
now in successful prosecution by the friends of colonization, for the re-
lief of a distressed class of our fellow men, over the *fruitless, impracticable,* and *dangerous theories,* of the advocates of immediate abolition.

We cheerfully commend your work to the public, and trust its general perusal will have a happy effect in removing unfavourable im-

pressions, and in increasing the interest which has recently been so signally manifested in the cause of colonization.

As citizens desiring the continuance and perpetuity of the peace, security, and happy union of our beloved country; as philanthropists anxious to promote the temporal and spiritual welfare of the people of colour, both bond and free; as Christians willing to pray and labour for the extension of the blessings of civilization and religion to benighted Africa; we do earnestly hope, that a cause, so blessed already by a benignant Providence, will continue to grow in the favour of this enlightened community, and its active advocates and supporters be furnished by its liberality with the means of accomplishing their benevolent and noble object.

We remain your Christian friends and coadjutors,

JAMES MILNOR, D. D.
WM. C. BROWNLEE, D. D.
THOS. DE WITT, D. D.

Dr. David M. Reese.

New-York, May 18, 1835.

From the Rev. N. Bangs, Editor of the Christian Advocate and Journal.

I have examined the Letters of Dr. D. M. Reese, addressed to the Hon. William Jay, in defence of the American Colonization Society, and in opposition to the Anti-Slavery Society, and believe them an ample and able refutation of the errors of the latter, as exhibited in Mr. Jay's unfortunate book, and a triumphant as well as timely vindication of the principles and proceedings of the American Colonization Society; and therefore most heartily and cordially recommend these Letters to the careful perusal and serious consideration of the American public.

NATHAN BANGS, D. D.

New-York, May 18, 1835.

PREFACE.

On the appearance of the "Inquiry" of the Hon. Mr. Jay, into the American Colonization and American Anti-Slavery Societies, I eagerly procured a copy, and read it throughout with mingled emotions of pain and pleasure. I was *pained* that so worthy a man should exhibit such evidence of ignorance of the subject on which he undertakes to enlighten the public; and still more, that such a man should descend from the dignity of his profession and character, to assail and satirize many of the ablest and best men of this nation, and that noblest enterprise of human benevolence, to which the American Colonization Society is consecrated; and this too on such questionable authorities, as those on which alone, he seems to have been dependent for his statements. But I found *pleasure* in this renewed demonstration, that the colonization scheme, though assailed by another of the champions among its foes, a man of talents, learning, and piety too, is, nevertheless, so firmly erect upon the immoveable foundation of light, and love, and truth; that it comes forth from this fiery ordeal, " like gold seven times tried," and retains all its brilliancy, purity, and strength, untarnished by the process, and triumphing in its own native and heaven-born sublimity.

Such were my impressions when I had finished its perusal; and a similar estimate of the utter impotency of the book, is, I have since learned, very generally entertained, by those of our fellow citizens, who are well informed in relation to the history and operations of the colonization enterprise. I therefore felt no disposition to attempt a reply, for, at that time, I confidently believed that the author had furnished, in the volume itself, abundant materials for his own refutation. I think so still, although I have yielded to the judgment of others, and consented again to engage in this controversy. I feel that I have no other qualification, than a conscientious attachment to the cause of colonization, because of an honest and deliberate persuasion, that it is one of supreme importance to the prosperity of my own country; of unmingled benevolence to the coloured population of this land, whether free or enslaved; and of rich and unspeakable promise to fallen, degraded, and heathenish Africa. But as many of our friends, who agree with me in my view of the harmlessness of the assault, which Mr. Jay's book contains, express their apprehensions, lest the magic of *his name* upon its title page, may mislead the " unlearned and unwary," and that multitudes of such may be taught to infer from our silence, that we cannot or dare not meet this " giant" in the field of discussion, they have judged it expedient, from these considerations, that a vindication of the society and its friends from the unjust accusations of the Hon. Judge, is imperiously called for, and, by common consent, the author of the present Letters has been urged to the unwelcome task.

That it has not been performed by another and an abler hand, is not less a matter of regret to myself, than it can be to others. For although I do not, in matters of conscience and duty, quail beneath the frowns of any foe, nor shrink from any measure of obloquy and reproach, which I am permitted to share with the wisest and purest men of this nation; yet, with the evidence of the spirit and temper of the present race of abolitionists, which experience has furnished, unless a man is doubly strong in his own conscious integrity of purpose, and prepared to endure the revilings, and brave the barkings of the whole kennel press, hired for the purpose; he will neither seek nor desire a conflict with such antagonists as gather around almost every anti-slavery periodical. It is perhaps well, however, that the party should be taught, in the present case, that this Goliath, in whom they glory, can be encountered by the " least among the hosts of our Israel," and, in the name of that God in whom we trust alone for the success of colonization, I go forth in this defensive war.

In the following Letters, it has been my design to treat the author with all proper respect, while I animadvert upon the contents of his book, with the same freedom with which he has treated the sentiments of colonizationists. I have therefore taken up the several chapters of his whole " Inquiry," and brought into view each of his prominent arguments, and the authorities on which he places most reliance; and in correcting his numerous mistakes, and exposing the contradictions and inconsistencies which abound in the volume, I have not designedly, in any instance, charged upon him an intention to deceive, but attribute his blunders to his recent associations, which have led him to fallacious sources for information, and perverted his own mind, so that, on this particular subject, he has become disqualified for sober thinking. And in offering this apology for the author of the Inquiry, which in candour and Christian charity is his due, we have another striking and melancholy proof of that mental and moral infatuation, which affords the deplorable evidence that the imputation of " fanati-

fulminating anathemas of anti-slavery lecturers, I would supplicate their mercy, and implore them to desist from their misplaced and misguided philanthropy. In the name of the afflicted free blacks of the north and the south, I would point them to the new and oppressive legislation which they have provoked by their ill-timed endeavours, and the rash impetuosity of their blind and mistaken zeal. And in behalf of the slaves of this land, I would invoke their humanity and religion, while groaning under already intolerable laws, and beseech them to withhold themselves from efforts, which in their results have already aggravated the number and severity of the privations and hardships which bondage inflicts.

But if my vindication of the Colonization Society disqualifies me from successfully urging my appeal, may I not ask Mr. Jay himself to pause, now that his book has gone forth for the vain though avowed purpose of the "*entire prostration*," the "utter extinction of the Colonization Society;"—now that he has proclaimed "unrelenting hostility," and beaten up for volunteers to "labour without rest and without weariness" for this great object; may I be permitted to ask him to pause and inquire, *Cui bono?* Suppose that the Colonization Society, were "utterly extinct," and that you had already effected its "entire prostration"—Let me ask what good purpose or result do your sanguine hopes allow you to anticipate, for the coloured race in the United States whether *free or slaves?* In that case the American Anti-Slavery Society would be your only hope of benefiting them, and where should we look for the first fruits of your success. Whose voice would then plead the cause of the oppressed in the slaveholding states? While your anti-slavery appeals from the forum and the press were "waking up the north," how many of the "millions of slaves in the south" would be thus emancipated, when your orators are excluded from every slaveholding state in the union, and your publications suffered to lie in the post-offices, or committed by thousands to the flames? And if you could not hope to benefit the slaves, by your labours in the north, what influence would you exert upon the *free* coloured population of the states south of the Potomac or even in Maryland or Delaware? Have not the events of the last two years, demonstrated that these northern anti-slavery efforts, in their effects upon the free blacks of the south, are "*evil, only evil, and that continually?*"

But shall we look to the non-slaveholding states, and estimate the character of the tree of "immediate abolition" by its "fruits?" What then have been the results upon the condition of the free coloured people in New-York? Within two brief years what scenes have been witnessed in this city and other sections of the state? Before the last year, an instance of insult to persons of colour in this city, under any circumstances, was exceedingly rare. They mingled in all our popular assemblages, and though often genteelly and even fashionably attired, their presence attracted little attention, and provoked no indignity. The intelligent and respectable among them, and there are many such in our city, were uniformly treated with kindness, and a tender sympathy for their depressed condition was generally felt among all classes of the community, which if suffered to grow, could not have failed to be most salutary in its results. Their friends among the whites, were rejoicing in the gradual and successful efforts made for their elevation, and the prospect of improving their condition encouraged the efforts which humanity and religion were making for their improvement. But in an evil hour, the spirit of Garrisonism was infused among these depressed people, and the result was first visible among themselves. From having been quiet and unassuming, as the better class of them proverbially were, they now began to assume an attitude of pride and independence. They were taught to regard themselves as perfectly equal to the whites in every aspect, and to attribute their separation, which long custom had rendered tolerable, as the fruits of robbery and oppression. Above all they were taught to abhor the Colonization Society, and to hate its members and friends with a perfect hatred. The idle and visionary hope of political and social equality in every relation, has been drilled into them, until they have lost the characteristics, which until now have been their safeguard from indignity and outrage. And accordingly these poor unfortunates have thence been exposed to outrages which else had never been committed. Apart from the sufferings inflicted upon the innocent and unoffending, during the *abolition riots* of the last year, they have since been insulted in numerous instances in the streets, and in public assemblages, until it has become dangerous for a coloured person male, or female, to be caught in a crowd. Their clothes have been torn off, they have been beaten and pelted with stones, and other acts of shameful cruelty have been committed upon them, such as were hardly ever known in this community. And why this change in the condition and prospects of the free coloured people of the north? Unquestionably it is the result of abolitionism, and the leaders of this party are responsible not only for their own acts, but for the altered bearing and conduct of these people themselves, so far as this may have provoked these outrages. From my soul I pity the delusion under which the coloured people of the north have been beguiled into circumstances so afflicting to themselves, by the " flattering unction" of these pseudo philanthropists.

The truth is becoming more and more apparent, that in the anti-slavery crusade against "vincible prejudice," they have created this prejudice where it *did not exist*, and they have fostered and strengthened it where it did, so that in the less intelligent portion of the community it has acquired an intensity by which it has been converted into cruelty and persecution. And this has been exhibited in so many instances, invariably and directly resulting from the measures of the Anti-Slavery Society, that intelligent men of colour are beginning to feel, in the language of one of them, that "these *friends* are digging a pit for our destruction." Still, however, multitudes of them are so infatuated by the anti-slavery delusion, that they continue to be inspired with the visionary hope, that they shall soon be elevated to perfect and universal equality with the white race.

I know that the members of the Anti-Slavery Society deceive themselves and others by the notion that if the Colonization Society were annihilated, these evils would no longer exist. They seem to think that but for the provision made by the society to transport to Africa such free persons of colour or manumitted slaves, as wish to go there, all the "*prejudice of caste*" would wither and die, and no farther obstacle exist in the way of "immediate and unconditional emancipation." But facts are altogether against this hypothesis. The cause of abolition is prosperous only in those sections of the south where colonization is popular, and no where is this cause so hindered as in those slaveholding states, where the society has but few friends. So obvious has been the influence of the Colonization Society in promoting actual abolition, that the true friends of the coloured race, would find a sufficient motive for supporting it in this single feature, if it accomplished nothing else either here or in Africa.

I will only add, that the discreet members of the Anti-Slavery Society, and there are doubtless many such, might find in the *class* of men with whom they are associated, ample reason to pause and ponder and retreat. It might not be easy to predict who would *not* become the votaries of abolitionism in any given place, where anti-slavery meetings were held; but one might readily prophesy who would certainly become such. Individuals and congregations, who are known to be *radicals*, in church or state ;—prone to *ultraism* on every subject with which they are connected, are the early converts to anti-slavery lecturers. Let the observation be made in any city, town, village, or congregation, where abolitionism has gained partizans, and it will be found, that however many from among other classes of the population may go over to the party, all those known by their general character to be enthusiasts, visionaries, fanatics, and radicals, in politics or morals, are sure to be included. And if there happen to be a church of any denomination, whose pastor and membership are proverbially given up to eccentricities in doctrine or to *ultra* measures, such church will prove a luxuriant garden for the growth of abolitionism. And though Mr. Jay seems to deprecate the fact that "infidels" are occasionally found among the friends of colonization, yet among his own associates, when he becomes better acquainted, he will find many such. One of these infidels in this city, who is an active friend of temperance as well as of immediate abolition, publicly and unblushingly avowed the sentiment very lately, that "neither the Anti-Slavery Society nor the Temperance Society, could ever succeed, unless *the Bible could be got out of the way!*" And when asked for an explanation, he falsely alleged that the Bible justified both *slavery and intemperance*, and referred to what he called Scripture proofs, which he said, while the people believed and reverenced, would be an insuperable obstacle to both these societies.

As I have attempted in the following Letters a vindication of the Colonization Society, because this is the chief object of his attack, and because I am in heart and action identified with that enterprise;—so I have been constrained to carry the war into the enemy's camp, and examine the principles, professions, and tendency of the American Anti-slavery Society, which is the subject of Mr. Jay's affection and eulogy.

Whether the "free discussion," which Mr. Jay invites, and which anti-slavery orators and presses *profess* to desire, and which is here attempted, shall be met with a spirit correspondent with their unanimous professions, remains to be seen. Should Mr. Jay think himself misapprehended, or should he be able to maintain any one of the heinous charges against the Colonization Society, which I have denied and repelled by unimpeachable testimony, the opportunity of free discussion is accessible to him, and the public will expect it. To such a reply, or to one from any other respectable source, I shall deem it a duty and pleasure to extend all due regard, and if I cannot sustain myself in the estimation of the discerning public, I am content to suffer the forfeiture. But while I shall feel bound to give respectful notice to any reply to my arguments, or any denial of the facts I record, let it be remembered that no reviling, calumny, or abuse aimed at my humble self, from any quarter, will meet any kind of notice. "I am doing a great work, and cannot *come down.*"

With these prefatory observations, I submit the following Letters to the judgment of the reader.

LETTERS

TO THE

HON. WILLIAM JAY.

LETTER I.

Sir,

Having read your "Inquiry into the character and tendency of the American Colonization and American Anti-Slavery Societies," and being convinced that the "character and ten dency" of your own book, demand an "inquiry," at this crisis in public feeling, which you have selected for its publication, I have chosen the form of letters to yourself, as that most con venient for my present purpose. The high regard I entertain for your general character and private worth, so favourably known, and deservedly appreciated among our fellow citizens, will entitle you to my respectful courtesy, and our mutual relationship as professors of a common Christianity, forbid that I should impeach your motives, or impugn either your integrity or benevolence.

The subject of your "Inquiry," however, is to every American citizen, of paramount importance, and to the Christian of absorbing interest. This you seem fully to estimate when you affirm in your Introduction, "If the claims of the American Colonization Society are *founded in truth*, they *cannot be resisted without guilt!*" page 7. And as you have written a volume in "resistance" of those claims, you have been obliged for the sake of your own consistency and justification, to at-

tempt the proof that they are not "founded in truth." You
will forgive me when I say, that you have failed to make ou
your case, not for lack of talents as a civiliın, or of skill as a
controversialist, or of learning as a judge, or of sincerity as a
Christian, but you have in the present case been self-deceived
by "want of information," and therefore you must permit me
in turn to "regret most sincerely, that a man possessing the
power of doing so much good, should ever, through WANT OF
INFORMATION, so grievously misapply it." p. 162.

In this "Introduction" to your book, which is the subject of
criticism in the present letter, your *first* paragraph makes the
astounding affirmation, that in the United States there are
2,245,144 slaves,* "*compelled* to *live without God*, and *to die
without hope*, by a people professing to reverence the obliga-
tions of Christianity." On such a fact, *if true*, an appeal
might be framed which would awaken heaven and earth, and
be "enough to make an angel weep." But is it true, that the
whole of our slave population "*live without God!*" and do
they all "*die without hope!*" and are they "*compelled*" to
do so by the inhuman monsters, who inhabit this nation?
Every reader who finds this hyperbole at the very threshold of

---

* This estimate of the whole number of slaves in the United States
on the 1st of January last, is made from the ratio of increase between
1820 and 1830. And as this description of *absolute* and *compulsory
heathenism*, is applied to them ALL, *without exception*, we shall look in
vain among the publications of the Colonization Society, for any similar instance of "*disparaging* the free blacks," and "*discouraging*
all efforts for their improvement," as the author's rhetorical flourish
here presents of "these millions of slaves." If such be truly the
character of the slaves, we should scarcely look for its avowal by an
advocate of "*immediate* abolition," since it presents "an apology for
slavery" which would justify the perpetuity of the system, unless they
could be *immediately* transformed by the process of emancipation, and
created anew by "instant abolition." The preparation of such hea-
thens for freedom, would indeed be a "triumph of *gradualism*," although it must be confessed that this picture of the intellectual and
moral degradation of 2,245,144 of our fellow beings, is enough not
only to annihilate the hopes of *immediate* abolitionists, but to fill the
hearts of the advocates of *gradual* emancipation itself with despair.
For if the whole of our slave population, at this day, be such as is
here represented, then may philanthropy and religion despair of a
remedy, and abandon their hopeless efforts. But on more mature reflection, Mr. Jay will acknowledge that he is mistaken, and lament
his own "want of information."

your book, must conclude that you commenced writing it in a state of mind and feeling not the best calculated for a grave "inquiry," or you would not thus indiscreetly make such a statement, so utterly "at variance with truth and Christianity," as you charitably charge against the Colonization Society on your 13th page.*

Suffer me to ask whether you had forgotten this sentence when you penned the 132d page of your book? How else do you say in that place, "We will not assert there are *no Christians* among the slaves, for we trust *there are some*." And again, "we suppose that 245,000 slaves possess *a saving knowledge of the religion of Christ!*" Do you mean to say that these 245,000 Christians, who "possess a saving knowledge of the religion of Christ, are *compelled* to *live without God*, and *die without hope?*" And can you persuade yourself, that such a number of Christians, who are the "light of the world," though they be in bonds, can fail to "let their light shine' among the slaves around them, and exert an influence which shall prevent all "these millions from being *kept* in *ignorance*, and *compelled* to *live without God* and *die without hope!*" If this be not undervaluing the Christian character, and depreciating the effect of Christian example, to an extent beyond any of the sentiments of the Colonization Society, against which you urge this objection, I fear that you will be grievously misinterpreted, for such will be the natural and le-

---

* The reader will, I am sure, be surprised and grieved at the extravagance of this sentiment. If it be true, that all the slaves of the United States, are "compelled to *live without God* and *die without hope*," what must be the immeasurable guilt and infamy which must attach to those who *inflict* this compulsion! Is Mr. Jay aware of the fact that thousands of slaveholders, are his fellow Christians, members of his own and other evangelical churches, in the southern and western states? Does he not know that very many of these are indefatigably employed in the religious instruction of their slaves, in encouraging and supporting *missions* to the plantations, on many of which churches are built for the slaves, by these slaveholders, where the gospel and the means of grace are faithfully supported at the expense of the planters? How then does he charge upon the owners of these slaves, the heinous guilt, the fiend-like crime, of "compelling their slaves to live without God and die without hope?" If he himself believes this statement, he must regard the entire south as worse than Sodom or Gomorrah, and every owner of slaves as a demon incarnate. I envy not, either his charity or his conscience.

gitimate conclusion of your readers. I confess it is a subject of surprise and affliction to me, that I am, thus early in my notice of your book, required to direct your attention to such glaring inconsistencies and mistakes. I did not expect it from the estimate I had formed of the author, and must deeply regret that the reader should find on the 5th page, this unfounded allegation, and then read on the 8th the profession of a "solemn recollection" on the part of the author, that "no deviation from truth can escape the notice and displeasure of Him unto whom all hearts are open and from whom no secrets are hid!" It is too painful to dwell on this unhappy evidence of the tendency of that malign influence which it is lamentably apparent, you have unconsciously received, by uncongenial proximity with the "spirit of anti-Colonization."

But your "want' of information" has led you into errors equally glaring in relation to the American Colonization Society, and this will appear to yourself and every reader in the very first mention you make of that institution, p. 7.

"A powerful institution is now in operation, which PROFESSES *to be not merely a* REMEDY FOR SLAVERY, but the ONLY remedy that *can be devised.*"

Now there are two statements in this brief sentence which I deny. The American Colonization Society does not "*profess* to be a remedy for slavery," nor does it profess to be the *only* one that "*can be devised.*" To each of these charges, in the language of the author in his vindication of his own associates; "the members of the Colonization Society plead NOT GUILTY, and desire to be tried by God and their country."

If these are the "claims," which you say are not "founded in truth," I ask you and the reader where are they made? Is it in the constitution of the society that it "*professes* to be not merely a remedy for slavery but the *only* one ?"—let us see.

EXTRACT FROM THE CONSTITUTION OF THE AMERICAN COLONIZATION SOCIETY.

"Art. I. This Society shall be called the American Society *for colonizing the free people* of colour of the United States.

"Art. II. The object to which its attention is to be EXCLUSIVELY directed, is to promote and execute a plan for colonizing (with their consent) the *free people* of colour residing in our country, in Africa, or such other place as congress shall deem most expedient."

Now it is obvious that this "powerful institution" "*professes*" nothing but what is contained in these two articles, and that the term "exclusively," renders it absolutely impossible that it should "*profess* to be a remedy for slavery, much less the *only* one." I would ask you then, sir, on what authority you make this allegation against the Colonization Society, and whether you are not here convicted of the precise accusation you bring on p. 147, against the Hon. Mr. Frelinghuysen, Chancellor Walworth, and David B. Ogden, Esq., by "not scrupling to hold up your fellow citizens and fellow Christians to the indignation of the public, on charges destitute of all specification, and unsupported by a particle of testimony ?"

I need not tell you, that it is utterly *absurd* to suppose that your allegation can have any foundation in truth. Who would believe a society, "*professing* to be a remedy for slavery," and yet defining their exclusive object to be the "colonizing the *free people* of colour." Still more absurd and ridiculous would be the *profession* of being the "*only* one that can be devised." What arrogance would this imply, in any society, or even "powerful institution," who should "profess" that no remedy "can be devised" but theirs, and especially when their constitution distinctly demonstrates that it *professes exclusively* a different object. And as I shall have occasion to show, you have yourself reprobated the society, for not deviating from its exclusive object. It is no vindication for this misrepresentation to allege, that some one or more of the friends of the society have regarded it in either of these lights, for your charge is distinctly that the society makes this *profession*, and this, as a friend of the society and in defence of the truth, I deny.*

But the next sentence in the same paragraph contains an

---

* In the language of another, we might repeat, "It is not a Missionary Society,—nor a society for the suppression of the slave trade, —nor a society for the improvement of the blacks,—nor a society *for the abolition of slavery ;*—but it is simply a society for establishing a colony on the coast of Africa; and so far as any of these other objects are attained by its efforts, they must be attained either as the means or as the consequences of establishing that colony." Did the society

equally egregious blunder, occurring, like the former, undoubted
ly, from "want of information." This "powerful institution,
you say, "appeals to religion and patriotism for those" pecu
niary aids, which it contends are *alone* wanting, to enable it
to transport our whole coloured population to Africa," &c.
Now I would respectfully ask for the evidence on which you
make this statement. Is it in the constitution, or in the Annual Reports of the managers? Does not the constitution
give it a palpable contradiction? Are "our whole coloured population" "*free* persons of colour?" And if they were, do they
all give their "*consent*" to go to Africa? How then could
the Colonization Society "contend," that money "*alone*" is
wanting, to "transport our whole coloured population," when
over two millions of them are *slaves*, which they do *not* transport, and nine tenths of the free withhold "*their consent*," and
therefore could *not* be colonized? But even if all were free,
and all consented to go, I ask, where is the evidence that the
society "contends" that even then, money "alone is wanting
to enable IT to transport our *whole coloured population?*"

It is to just such misrepresentations, and misapprehensions
arising from "want of information," or erroneous information,
that the lamented Wilberforce* withdrew his confidence from
the cause; and to the same source is it to be ascribed, if, as
you say, the American Colonization Society "is regarded with
abhorrence by almost the whole religious community of Great
Britain." When such a man as Wm. Lloyd Garrison was sent
to England, mainly on the errand of denouncing the motives,
character, and tendency of the society, and when even a British philanthropist, in rebuking him for vilifying his country,
was constrained to say, "Mr. Garrison *distorts meanings,*—
fastens the *speeches of individuals* on the society,—quotes
partially,—*conceals* explanations,—*exaggerates,*—*clamours,*

---

ever "profess to be a remedy for slavery and the only one?" I submit to Mr. Jay whether he has not here overlooked the *ninth commandment of the decalogue.* Let reason and conscience answer.

* Dr. Hodgkin, of London, in his able pamphlet, says, that "Wilberforce continued to avow his approbation of the American Colonization Society, notwithstanding the attacks and insinuations of its
adversaries, until near the period of his lamented death, when the
exparte statements of those who knew the importance of his authority
obtained a triumph, the achievement of which confers no honour."

—and *cants*," what could be expected other than that just so far as he was believed in Great Britain, the society and the nation would be viewed with "abhorrence?" His pamphlet contained ten specific accusations against the society, most heinous and anti-Christian in their nature; and although the society and its friends plead *not guilty* to each of them, and have continued to the present, "solemnly" to pronounce their author to be a calumniator, yet I regret to perceive, that the most of these offences are alleged against the society in your book, and in some instances fortified by quotations even from Garrison himself! But suffer me to adopt your own language, and ask, "What proof is offered? Nothing, absolutely nothing is offered, but naked assertion. Is this equitable? Is it doing to others as you would wish others to do to you?"

I shall, in my next letter, notice the first chapter in your book. and I regret to say, that it abounds in exceptionable and erroneous matter no less than your brief introduction, and believe me, my animadversions upon your "inquiry," are offered "more in sorrow than in anger," and you must not account me an enemy because I tell you the truth.

With due respect,

Yours, &c.

LETTER II.

Sir,

Your first chapter, on the "Origin, Constitution and Character of the American Colonization Society," will be the subject of the present letter.   And I cannot withhold the expression of my regret, that your deplorable "want of information" has led you into an error, for which, I am sure, your own candid reconsideration of your book, will inspire you with repentance, however unavailing it may be, in respect to the influence it has already exerted, and will continue to exert, wherever it is read. I allude now to the obvious attempt you make to connect a "resolution of the Legislature of Virginia," with the "*origin*" of the American Colonization Society. Your object is so obviously to identify the organization of the society with slavery and slaveholders, that you connect these two events, which you ought to know, have no more kindred relation, than your own book has with either of them. The *coincidence* in the date of the Virginia resolution, 23d December, 1816,* and that of the organization of the American Colonization Society, is obviously pointed at, when you say, "within *a few days* of the date of this resolution, a meeting was held at Washington, to take *this very subject* into consideration. It was composed *almost*

---

* It is singularly unfortunate for Mr. Jay's object, that the meeting held in Washington, "within a few days" of this date, "to take *this very subject* into consideration," had the priority in point of time, to the Virginia resolution, for it was held on the 21st of December, 1816, two days *before* that resolution, and not, as erroneously insinuated, *after* it. If then he had been willing to express the truth *chronologically*, he would have *first* related the meeting of the "slaveholders" in Washington, and then the *subsequent* resolution of the Virginia Legislature, as occurring "*within a few days of the date*"of the former. But this would have reversed the impression designed to be made upon the reader's mind, yet the truth required it.

entirely of *southern gentlemen ;*" and after naming Judge Washington, Mr. Clay, and Mr. Randolph, you say, the meeting "resulted in the organization of the American Colonization Society !" Such disingenuousness and uncandid distortion of facts, especially with the design of attributing the origin of the society to the Virginia resolution referred to, was hardly to be expected from such a man as Mr. Jay.

But who would imagine, that you could have professed to give the ' *origin* of the American Colonization Society," and yet, never mention the *name* of its illustrious and excellent founder ? This were to betray as great "want of information" as a man would exhibit, if he were to pretend to write the history of his country, and never once name the "father of his country." And yet, such is the attitude in which you have been placed by the "bad advisers" into whose hands you have unhappily fallen. Even Garrison ! pronounces the name of ROBERT FINLAY with respect and veneration, and declares him and many of his followers to be " men of piety, benevolence, and moral worth." Indeed, in the crusade *he* has been prosecuting against the society, when he speaks of " *those who planned* the American Colonization Society," he has a " lucid interval to his madness," and is constrained by reason or conscience, to say, that "some of them, *undoubtedly*, were actuated by a benevolent desire to *promote the welfare of our coloured population*, and *could never have intended* to countenance oppression !"   But alas, we look to your book in vain for any other name in connexion with the "origin" of this scheme of philanthropy but those of "slaveholders," or those whom you stigmatize with this epithet. Let me ask, is this fair ? Is it candid ? Is this an exemplification of the "golden rule ?" Because that holy man, ROBERT FINLAY, the founder of the society, and his devoted companions, in this "work of faith," the excellent *Caldwell*, and the pious *Mills*,—because these were not " *slaveholders*," you carefully omit to mention their *names*, in your professed history of the "origin" of the society ; while other names are repeated for this single reason, that they were slaveholders. I charitably hope, that your "want of information" may prove a sufficient apology to your conscience and your God.

You next quote the first two articles of the constitution,

against which you protest, because you allege the want of a
"*preamble*, setting forth the motives which led to its adoption,
and the sentiments entertained by its authors." Has the American Bible Society any such preamble to its constitution? or
has that of the American Anti-Slavery Society, which you so
zealously advocate? The "*motives and sentiments*" of the
authors, are explicitly declared in the constitution itself, in all
these societies, and "the want of a preamble" is an objection
whicn has as much force against the one as the other of
them. Indeed, the method of prefixing a "preamble" to con-
stitutions, is now, for the most part, *obsolete*, and is very rarely
adopted any where. This objection, then, is entirely unfounded, though you most uncharitably attribute the "omission of
all avowal of motives to *design*."

The effect which you allege, as produced by this *designed.
omission*, is that of "securing the co-operation of three classes," whom you designate as benevolent men, interested slaveholders, and cruel persecutors, and you affirm that, "there is *no
one principle of duty or policy*," recognised by the constitution. How you could make this assertion in the face of the
two articles you quote, is indeed "passing strange." Is not
"promoting and executing a plan for colonizing the free people
of colour" one "principle of *duty*?" and is not another *principle*
of duty found in the word "exclusively" in relation to the single object, and still another, in the words "with their consent,"
which is tantamount to an assurance, that "forcible expatriation" can never receive the countenance of the society. And
is there "no one principle of *policy*" in the reference to "Africa, or such other place as *congress shall deem most expedient*," and "in *co-operation* with the general government and
such of the states as may adopt regulations on the subject?"
These are the "motives and sentiments" of the society, as
avowed in their constitution, and in precisely the location in
which a similar avowal of other "motives and sentiments" is
found in the constitution of the American Anti-Slavery Society,
viz. in the second article, and not in the "preamble," for there
is none in either.

As to the "heterogeneous multitude who have entered the
Colonization Society, because its doors are thrown open to all,"

the only difference consists in the fact, that in the Anti-Slavery
Society, slaveholders are excluded. This exclusion is, how
ever, more nominal than real; for, though slaveholders are pro
hibited from becoming members, yet *slave-traders* are not, *i.*
they "*consent* to the principles of the constitution, and contri
bute to the funds." I say nothing of the incongruity of form
ing a society professedly against slavery, and yet excluding
from its portals the only persons who can practise abolition
For even if a slaveholder consents to the principles of the con
stitution, and pays to the funds, yet he cannot be a member o.
the society, however anxious to get rid of his slaves, until the
Colonization Society first transport his slaves to Liberia, ana
thus render him eligible for membership in the Anti-Slavery
Society. If a moiety of the sums expended upon Anti-Slavery
agents, and in the support of the Anti-Slavery press, were paiu
over to the treasury of the American Colonization Society, they
would render very many benevolent and pious *slaveholders* eligible to membership, who for want of it, will probably never
be able to obtain admission, nor cease to be slaveholders.

But your next complaint against the constitution, is, that so
great a variety of characters, influenced by an equal variety o.
motives, good and bad, leads to "a lamentable compromise of
principle." To show that this is what logicians call a *non sequi-
tur*, it will only be necessary to refer to the British and Foreign
Bible Society, an Institution whose principles and practice
challenge the admiration of the world. Its "*single* object" is
the "circulation of the Holy Scriptures, without note or comment." It makes no requisition of "motives or sentiments" in
"a preamble," nor does it require any test of membership, for
every slaveholder on the earth may be a member. It contains
as great an "amalgamation of characters and motives," and
"the doors of the society being thrown *open to all*, a heterogeneous multitude has entered, and within its portals, men are
brought into contact, who, in the ordinary walks of life, are separated by a common repulsion." In short, all that you say in
this strain, against the American Colonization Society, lies
with equal force against that great and good institution, the
British and Foreign Bible Society. But would you thence allege, a "lamentable compromise of principle." Because Cal-

vinists and Armınians, Pædo Baptists, and Anti-Pædo Baptists, High Church and Low Church, Trinitarians and Unitarians, Orthodox and Heterodox, a "heterogeneous multitude," have entered its portals, and agreed to unite in the "*single object*" of the society, however they may be "separated by a common repulsion" on all other subjects,—would you be found in league with Irving and others, in denouncing that noble enterprise of human benevolence, the extent of whose usefulness is by this very "heterogeneousness," tenfold greater than it could otherwise be? Your avowed attachment to the American Bible Society, founded on similar principles, forbids the supposition, and yet you are yourself associated in that society with *slaveholders by the thousand.*

But I have said, that you reprobate the society because of its *exclusive* character, as appears in this chapter, in which you complain, that "the constitution contains no allusion to slavery." How then did you charge it with "professing to be a remedy for slavery." If this charge were true, you might justly complain, that "its constitution contains no allusion to slavery," for this would indeed involve an inconsistency. As it is, however, this fact is in itself a refutation of all you have said on this subject.

Your assertion, that the silence of the constitution with respect to manumission, "is not permitted to interpose the slightest obstacle to a *unanimous*, vigorous, and persevering opposition to present manumission," is entirely destitute of proof, and that the American Colonization Society either "deprecates the emancipation of slaves, or censures all who propose it," is palpably in contravention of multiplied facts, of some of which, your own book furnishes the evidence, as I shall hereafter have occasion to demonstrate. The tirade here indulged in, to show that it is *constitutional* to denounce the *foreign* traffic, and declare it piratical, and at the same time *unconstitutional*, to condemn the *domestic* slave trade, or labour for its suppression;—and the illiberal insinuation, that these inconsistencies are "expedients to conciliate the slaveholders," will also be noticed in a subsequent letter.

With due respect,
Yours, &c.

LETTER III.

Sir,

THE following paragraph in your book, I regard as one of the most extraordinary examples of "at least doubtful morality," to use your own language, that I have ever seen from the pen of a good man, and it is one which calls for a specific examination.

" To hold up the *free blacks* to the *detestation* of the community is constitutional!—to recommend them to the *sympathy* of Christians, to propose *schools* for their instruction, plans for encouraging their *industry*, and efforts for their *moral and religious* improvement, would be such a flagrant departure from the 'exclusive' object of the society, that NO MEMBER has hitherto been *rash enough* to make the attempt! At the same time, it is quite constitutional to *vindicate the cruel laws* which are crushing these people to the dust, and to show that the oppression they suffer is an 'ordination of providence.' "

As a number of these statements will come up in another form as we proceed, I will at present only offer my remonstrance against the strange and unaccountable asseveration, that "*no member* of the Colonization Society has hitherto been rash enough to make the attempt to propose *schools* for the instruction, plans for the encouragement of the *industry*, or efforts for the *moral and religious* improvement of the *free blacks !*" And now, sir, allow me to ask you whether you do not know, that until two or three years ago, the efforts made, plans proposed, and schoo's sustained, for the benefit of the free blacks in every part of the United States, were for the most part, the result of the personal exertions and liberality of members of the Colonization Society ? Who are the men who have borne the burden and heat of the day, in the various Manumission Societies in Pennsylvania, New-York, New-

Jersey, Massachusetts, Connecticut, Rhode Island, even when
the most of these were slave states? Are they not the
men, in numerous instances, at least, who are members and
friends of the Colonization Society? Are there not eight free
manumission schools in the city of New-York alone, which
have chiefly been sustained by colonizationists? Who has
built, purchased, and sustained churches for the "moral and religious improvement of the free blacks" in every part of this
country? Let this investigation be made, and you will be
ashamed of the injustice you have unwittingly done to the
members of the Colonization Society.

I might here refer you to the numerous day and Sunday
schools for the free blacks, which colonizationists have organized
and conducted, many of which are now in successful operation,
and some of which have been broken up by the benevolent efforts
of the anti-slavery people, in creating prejudice against teachers,
after years of devotion to the best interests of these people, by
denouncing them to their scholars, as members of the Colonization Society, and, therefore, "wolves in 'sheep's clothing.'"*

But suffer me to refer you to the recent purchase of the Presby-

---

* A striking illustration exists in New-York, in the history of a
Sabbath school for coloured people, adults and children, under the
patronage of the Rev. Dr. Milnor, of this city, and superintended for
a number of years by Mr. Taylor. In this school, numbering between three and four hundred scholars, many have been taught to
read, some in advanced life, and the moral and religious improvement of the scholars was most gratifying to the friends of humanity,
and until the introduction of the Anti-Slavery mania, its prosperity
and success continued without interruption. But during the last year,
it was ascertained that the superintendant would not join the Anti-
Slavery Society, and it was therefore concluded, *de facto*, by some of
its members, that he was a colonizationist, although he has never become a member of any Colonization Society. Nevertheless, as he
did not become an *anti-colonizationist*, and declined having that
subject introduced into his Sabbath school, the most diligent and
persevering efforts were used by the abolitionists to alienate the
scholars, and estrange their confidence from the school and its inde-
fatigable teachers, whose practical benevolence had been demonstrated
by years of faithful devotion to this work. The result of such *benevolent* efforts has been seen, in the diminution of the number of scholars from 400 to 40 or 50, and the *persecution* of those who remain
The bitter and uncompromising opposition to this school, has probably
arisen from the fact that the Rev. Dr. Milnor, the pastor of the church
by whom it is sustained, is an officer of the city Colonization Society.

terian church in Frankfort-street, New-York, occupied by a
congregation of free blacks, under the pastoral care of the Rev.
Mr. Wright. When the Committee of the "New-York Pres-
bytery," went through the city, soliciting donations for this laudable object, begging from door to door, until they obtained between nine and twelve thousand dollars; who were the men
whose subscriptions of from one to five hundred dollars, gave
evidence of their interest in the moral and religious improvement of these people? I answer, they were, with scarcely an individual exception, members and friends of the Colonization
Society. Your friend and fellow labourer, the Rev. Dr. Cox,
then a colonizationist, was one of the committee at first, though
his anti-slavery occupations, since his conversion to that creed,
have rendered it inconvenient to continue to act with the committee. He can tell you, however, if he has not forgotten it,
who were the men, who *refused* to contribute to this scheme of
benevolence, and excused themselves on the *anti-slavery* pretext, that they disapproved of providing *separate* places of worship for the "free blacks," lest it should foster *prejudice*, and
insisted that they ought to be provided for in our own churches,
"*without distinction of colour.*"

The subscription book may yet be seen, and you would be
constrained after examining it, for yourself, to retract your
cruelly unjust accusation, that "no member of the Colonization Society" has attempted "efforts for the moral and religious improvement of the free blacks," if conscience and duty
did not compel you to render restitution to those, whose names
and memory you have thus rudely assailed. Let me not be
understood to impugn your motives, or impeach your sincerity,
but only to allege your lamentable "want of information" as
the obvious cause of your mistakes.

From such erroneous opinions as your recent associations
have led you to form, and the perverted views you have thence
taken of this whole subject, it is no marvel that your zeal
should be enkindled against a society whose principles and
practice you have so grievously misunderstood. Hence you
deliberately charge upon "good men and good Christians" the
"adoption of *expediency*, as the standard of right and wrong,

in the place of the revealed will of God.'—"*opinions* and *practices* inconsistent with *justice* and *humanity!*" and under the *demoralizing influence* " of colonization," you allege against these "good men and good Christians" that they "advance in its behalf opinions at variance with truth and Christianity!" Truly you are constrained to admit, that "these are grave assertions, and very extraordinary ones!" and our readers will see in the sequel what proof you present in the form of "authentic facts." It must be obvious, however, to yourself, that in this your "general statement of the case against the society," you have included in your indictment so many counts that impeach the integrity of its members, that if a moiety of them be substantiated, so far from being "good men and good Christians," they are, *en masse*, worthy of the reprobation of every friend of humanity, "fellows not fit to live."

And now, sir, these "grave *assertions* and very extraordinary ones," as you admit them to be, involve the personal and Christian character of men, distinguished at home and abroad for their station, reputation, and usefulness. The gentlemen whose names you unceremoniously introduce into your book, are not only regarded as Christian gentlemen, but many of them as Christian divines, whose estimable character and private worth, has made them known and respected in every part of our own country, and equally so in every Christian nation on the earth. And yet, against these men, your book alleges not merely a "lamentable compromise of principle," but you ascribe to them the attributes of "stupidity," "ignorance," "prejudice," "inconsistency," "persecution," "cruelty," "inhumanity," "duplicity," and opinions and practice "at variance with truth and Christianity." You represent the Hon. Theodore Frelinghuysen, Chancellor Walworth, David B. Ogden, Esq., Right Rev. Dr. Hawks, the venerable Bishop White, Rev. Dr. Beecher, and all others among the respectable divines, statesmen, patriots, and Christians, who belong to the Colonization Society, as men utterly unworthy of the affection or confidence of the "friends of humanity and religion," and you call upon such for "*unrelenting hostility*" against them and the cause with which they are identified.

Wherever your book shall go, its readers will be prepared, if they believe your accusations, to look upon these excellent men, with loathing and "abhorrence," and these American divines and Christians, when they visit England or France, as the agents of the churches, and the representatives of our benevolent institutions, will be viewed, so far as your testimony can produce this effect, as the abettors of a system of "abominable persecution." And the responsibility for all this "obloquy and reproach" being poured upon "good men and good Christians," as you inconsistently call them, you have voluntarily assumed. Where they are known, they are shielded from all your shafts, by their established integrity ; and I need not tell you, that pure and exalted as your own character is admitted to be at home, these gentlemen, whom you assail, are in every respect your equals in the estimation of the Christian public, for all that is "lovely and of good report," and that the endorsement of your name to this attack upon their reputations, will be utterly insufficient to stain their characters, or abstract from them any measure of the public confidence. But at a distance from home, in our own and other countries, the accusations of your book cannot but inflict upon these your "Christian brethren" unmerited injuries, which you can never repair, and wounds, which you can never heal. If this consideration can afford you consolation, either living or dying, you are welcome to its exclusive enjoyment.

I propose to continue my correspondence until I shall examine the whole of the "special pleading," which you have thought necessary in the case. To each and every one of your charges, the society and its friends plead "*not guilty,*" and as we are now before the American people, and you and I are members of that bar, and engaged as opposite counsel, though volunteers in the case, I shall submit to the court and jury a brief analysis of the evidence you present, and claim the verdict which reason and conscience shall approve. In one respect, I may, without arrogance, lay claim to stand on equal footing with yourself. I mean, in the honest conviction that my client, the American Colonization Society, is innocent of the crimes and high misdemeanours, for which you have drawn the indictment. And while I award to you an equal conscientiousness in conducting the prosecution, and a full persuasion that my client is guilty and ought to be condemned, I shall submit the case to God and my country, and personating my client, I would exclaim with the great Apostle of the Gentiles, " If I be an offender, or have committed any thing worthy of death, I refuse not to die."

With due respect,
Yours, &c.

LETTER IV.

Sir,

Your second chapter will constitute the subject of the present letter, and although it is extended through 38 pages of your book, yet there is so much of irrelevant and technical matter contained in it, that I shall purposely decline any very minute or detailed controversy, except in reference to a few points directly bearing on the subject.

After denying that there is any thing *necessarily benevolent* in the exclusive object of colonizing the free people of colour with their own consent, you charge upon the society, "the *policy* of aggravating prejudice against the free blacks," and with using "*unchristian language* in regard to this unhappy and oppressed portion of their fellow men." To sustain this heinous allegation, a number of extracts are given from speeches delivered by friends of the society, and other printed documents. As in my subsequent letters, I may have occasion to apply the *lex talionis*, to the society you represent, I shall waive the legitimate objection often made by the society, against being held responsible for the sentiments held or expressed by its real or supposed friends. These may be injudicious and often erroneous, and according to no honest rules of testimony can any body of men be held accountable for every expression used by its individual members, and especially when detached and dismembered sentences are selected, often without accompanying qualifications, which essentially modify and even change the speaker's meaning. But admitting that the extracts you make do prove, as you design, that their authors "aggravate the prejudice against the free blacks," even by the use of "unchristian language," it is only necessary for me to prove by the same kind of evidence, that other and opposite sentiments are held and expressed in a different spirit, and it will then be in proof, that the society is as much represented in the one case as the other; that is, *responsible for neither*. Whenever a speaker or writer introduces any sentiment other than in favour of the exclusive object of " colonizing the free people of colour with their own consent," he alone is responsible, and not the society whose cause he advocates. A Unitarian will advocate the distribution of the Bible, with the avowed motive to propagate his doctrines ; so also will a Universalist, a Baptist, a Calvinist, an Arminian, and each will urge upon his congregation the duty of promoting the circulation of the Scriptures, for the purpose of advancing the doctrines of his particular sect.   But did you ever dream that the Bible Society was accountable for the varied and even opposite arguments of its professed friends. But an attempt to prove the American Bible Society to be a Unitarian Society, because those who deny the divinity of Christ, profess to expect their doctrines to be propagated by the circulation of " the Scriptures without note or comment," would not be more preposterous, than to argue that the American Colonization Society is unchristian, because " unchristian language" may have been used by some of its friends.   All that would be necessary to vindicate the Bible Society in the case supposed, would be to show, that " Trinitarians" employed opposite sentiments and arguments in behalf of the society ;—and I shall now proceed to show that other friends of colonization have entertained and expressed essentially different language and sentiments from those you have presented.   And first let me refer you to one of the resolutions adopted at the annual meeting in January, 1833.

Resolved, that the *free people of colour* throughout the United States, be assured, that this society had its origin in the most *benevolent* desires towards them ; that its object is to promote their *happiness and usefulness ;* and that it believes this can *best be done* by gradually separating them (*with their own consent*) from the white race, and establishing them in a situation where they may enjoy those *privileges to which they are entitled by nature and their Creator's will."* 16th *Annual Report.*

Is this calculated to " aggravate prejudice?"

" We should direct our efforts to the *improvement of our coloured population* more than we have done, and thus fit them for the responsible duties of colonists among the pagans of their colour." "I know the history of the cause of colonization, it originated in the best and purest motives." *Rev. Gardiner Spring, D. D.*

Is this unchristian language?

The cause of colonization is the safest, truest, and most efficient auxiliary of freedom, "*under existing circumstances.*" *Constitution of Maryland in Liberia.*

"It is the opinion of this body that African colonization is eminently calculated to benefit a *long persecuted*, and *deeply injured* race, by furnishing to the *free people of colour* an opportunity to escape from the *oppression* which *they suffer* in this country," &c. *Resol. Gen. Assem. Presb. ch. May,* 1832.

"That the colonization of the people of colour of the United States on the coast of Africa, will not only promote their own temporal *freedom* and *happiness*, but tend to their *moral improvement*," &c. *Address of Maryland State Col. Society.*

Now in these several quotations it will be seen that colonizationists speak and write without "unchristian language," and discover no "policy of aggravating prejudice against the free blacks." So far from this, the society and its friends commiserate the depressed condition of this class, lament the extent of that prejudice, which under present circumstances forbid all hope of their elevation, and advocate the cause from a benevolent desire to promote their happiness and usefulness. How mistaken then is your declaration, that "*the society excuses and justifies* the *oppression* of the free negroes, and *the prejudices against them*," p. 17. It is true you have found some detached sentences of speeches and other publications by colonizationists, which are made to have the semblance of such tendency, though some of the authors would protest against this use made of their words, as doing them injustice. They have stated the depressed condition of the free people of colour, in slaveholding and non-slaveholding states, in strong language, and represented the unconquered and unconquerable nature of that prejudice which perpetuates their depression. But not one, even among those whom you have quoted, either "excuses or justifies it,"—and I marvel greatly that you should give your name to such a charge without other and better evidence. In-

deed your extract from the Address of the Connecticut Colonization Society is most unfairly made, for you leave out the following sentence, which is part of the same paragraph you employ, and proves that neither "excuse nor justification" is attempted. The address speaks of " things as they *are* and not
as they *might*, or *ought to be*," and hence uses the following
language, in direct connexion with what you have quoted, and
which any reader will see, essentially varies its meaning, and
contradicts your interpretation.

" The African *in this country* belongs by birth to the very
lowest station in society : and from that station he can never
rise, be his talents, his enterprise, his virtues, what they may.
They [the free negroes] constitute a class by themselves, a
class out of which no individual *can be elevated*, and below
which none can be depressed. And this is the *difficulty*, the
invariable and *insuperable* difficulty, in the way of every
scheme for their *benefit*. Much can be done for them—much
has been done, but still they are, and in this country *always
must be, a depressed and abject race*." And hence " it is
taken for granted that *in present circumstances*, any effort to
produce a *general* and *thorough* amelioration in the character
and condition of the free people of colour, must be to a great
extent, fruitless. In every part of the United States there is a
broad and impassable line of demarcation between every man
who has one drop of African blood in his veins and every other
class in the community."

I put it to your candour, sir, whether these sentiments, in
their original connexion with the extract you have dismembered, either excuse or justify the oppression and prejudice to
the existence of which they attest. I take it for granted that
you admit the truth of the description here given, for the complaints in your own book against " oppression and prejudice"
are all unfounded, unless all that is here stated is *true*. And
its truth being established, this " narrative of facts" on the side
of colonization, is not more justly chargeable than is your own,
with the guilt of " excusing or justifying it."

But you next assert, that " the society *discourages* all attempts to *improve the condition* of the free blacks." Allow
me again to lament the deplorable " want of information"

which has led you to a repetition of this often refuted calumny. The quotations you make are utterly irrelevant ; and in signal refutation of all you have written to sustain your position, I invite your attention to the following.

"Colonization tends to *improve* the character and *elevate* the condition of the free people of colour, and thus to take away one standing and very influential argument against individual emancipation and general abolition." "*Elevate the character* of the free people of colour,—let it be seen that *they are men indeed*—let the *degrading associations which follow them be broken up* by the actual *improvement* of their character as a people, and negro slavery must rapidly wither and die." *Christian Spectator*, a "religious colonization paper."

The following extract, in point, is from the same journal. "The success of colonization will not only bless the colonists, but will *react to elevate the standing of those who remain behind;* and from beyond the Atlantic there will come a light to beam upon the degradation of the negroes in America."

Such are the expressed designs of colonizationists, and not a shadow of testimony is, or can be furnished, that the society or its distinguished members, have ever "discouraged attempts to improve the condition of the free blacks."

The most imposing evidence which this chapter contains, is in your strictures upon the case of Miss Crandall, and her far famed "Canterbury School," the "Black Act of Connecticut," and the "charge of Judge Dagget" of that state. As these matters are entirely irrelevant, I shall not discuss them here, since neither are directly or indirectly connected with the Colonization Society, as every reader will perceive, notwithstanding your laboured attempt to impute them all to the society, and its friends. In the name of colonization I utterly repel the insinuation, that these difficulties in Connecticut originated in the doctrines or measures of the American Colonization Society, nor would any of them have occurred, had the *Anti-Slavery Society* never existed. They afford abundant confirmation, however, of the existence of the "prejudice and oppression" which the society deplore while they record, and demonstrate that the statements of the Colonization Society in relation to the invincible character of this prejudice are neither misrepresented nor overrated.

Forgive me, sir, when I say that your laboured attempt to identify the laws of the slave states, and the recent commotions in the non-slaveholding states with the Colonization Society, afford ample and melancholy demonstration of your own sentiment expressed on your 46th page, that " even good men are subject to *erroneous opinions* and *unwarrantable prejudices.*" In my next I shall notice the subject of " compulsory emigration."

With due respect,
Yours, &c.

LETTER V.

Sir,

THE running title of your book for several pages is, "Compulsory Emigration." This charge you bring against the society was hardly to be expected, when their constitution which you quote is so explicit in its contradiction. But it is in vain that the society points to the "second article," in which it is distinctly avowed that it will colonize the free people of colour only with *their own consent*, and that this is its object, "exclusively" its only object. You even ridicule this provision, by denominating the phrase "their own consent," *three talismanic words!* and you call the constitutional argument which the society urges on these words, a *specious* one, and allege that the society "transports negroes whose *consent*, they well know has been extorted from them by the most abominable persecution!"

And what is the proof you offer? Let us see.

The slave states, you say, "oppress these people, and keep them in ignorance and degradation." And pray, is the Colonization Society to be held responsible for the acts of the several state legislatures, most of which were passed before the society was in being? On what principle of justice or equity can you make this appear? Surely it is not sufficient to show that these same legislatures have passed resolutions approving of the society, and its objects. But nevertheless on such evidence alone, you do attempt to convict the society of violating their constitution by "compulsory emigration." Not merely the laws which each state in its sovereign capacity sees fit to adopt, and the decisions of their courts, but even the speeches of members in the several houses of delegates, are all charged upon the "benevolent colonization system," and you go so far as to affirm that "all look to the Colonization Society as the instrument, by which the *forcible expulsion* of the free negroes is to be effected!" and you add, " Nor do they look in vain!"

And here in your own language, page 28, I am constrained to say, "there are occasions on which it is treason to truth and honour, if not to religion, to suppress our indignation," nor can I shrink from the expression of my opinion, that your "unwarrantable prejudices" have led you to a course "inconsistent with either truth or Christianity." I shall not refer to the cruelty and injustice of reprobating the society for the circumstances which followed the Southampton massacre, and the censure attempted to be fixed on the society for removing those who begged for a passage to Liberia, to escape from the inhumanity of their relentless persecutors, goaded to unwonted violence by the scenes of blood they had witnessed, but I will proceed to prove from official documents, that it is *not true* that the Colonization Society ever countenanced or encouraged coercion, but has rigidly and universally disclaimed, from the beginning, all "compulsory emigration." Let the reader look at the following conclusive evidence on this point.

" They [the society] do *not intend*, and *they have not the inclination*, if they possessed the power, to *constrain* the departure of any free man of colour from America." *Third Annual Report.*

" Nathaniel Paul, an intelligent and well informed North American of colour, who is decidedly opposed to the Colonization Society, *does not attempt* to press this accusation, as *believed*, either by himself or his brethren. He only states their *fears* that COERCION may *hereafter* be resorted to!" Dr. *Hodgkin's Inquiry.*

" I cannot find in any of the writings of our opponents, the *slightest attempt at proof*, that the society has, in any instance, violated its principle. They do not so much as hint, at the occurrence of *one example* of a coloured individual having been conveyed from America to Africa, under the auspices of the society, *against his own wish*." *Ibid.*

" But is there nothing good in the American Colonization Society ? Yes, there is. For the few coloured people who *prefer* leaving their native country, and emigrating to Africa, it is unquestionably a great blessing!" *Charles Stewart's*

Letter to the " Herald of Peace." This is the more valuable, as the testimony of an implacable enemy of the cause, who does not insinuate the charge we are considering.

In one of the Annual Reports the society officially declares:

" We *disavow and reprobate* every *coercive measure*, we discard all restraint, we ask no bounties—we solicit *no com pulsion* by which to produce emigration."

Such are the proofs which the " Reports," to which you seem to have had access, and other documents, furnish in contradiction of your allegation; and yet, sir, on the 52d page of your book, you say,

" In sixteen years, 2162 have been sent away, some at first vo- luntarily, but *many of them* through COERCION." And is it too much to say, that you are bound to sustain your veracity by naming the time, place, and persons thus coerced, or to admit that you have here transgressed tne ninth commandment. It will not do for you to refer to the absurd and unfeeling speech of Mr. Broadnax, in the Virginia House of Delegates, on a bill which that body *rejected,*—nor to the persecutions subsequent to the insurrection of Southampton, for neither of these have any, the least connexion with the society. And as it is against the society, as such, that you charge "compulsory emigration," you are again called upon as in duty bound to sustain, or retract it. Let me commend to your sober reflection the sentiment you express on the 147th page of your book: as you are yourself of " the legal profession, you are aware of the importance of precision in all charges of a criminal nature, you would not, sitting as a criminal judge, permit the *merest vagabond* to be put on his defence on a vague charge of stealing, but would quash any indictment that did not specify the time and place of the offence, and the property alleged to be stolen; yet you do not scruple to hold up your fellow citizens and fellow Christians to the indignation of the public on a charge destitute of all specification, and unsupported by a particle of testimony."

I might here add, you have yourself furnished evidence in refutation of your own accusation, in the extract you make from the New-York Colonization Society's Address. " We say to the free blacks, we think you may improve your condition by going thither, but if you *prefer* remaining here, you will be protected and treated with kindness," and this you insert under the head of "compulsory emigration." It is true you contrast it with the language of the same society, when addressing the legislature, and attempt to fix upon them the same crime of "*coercing* their *consent* to go to Africa*," with what consistency every reader will judge.

But you are so indiscriminate in your censoriousness, that you quote the language of Mr. Gurley's letter, and pervert a sentiment purely the dictate of humanity, to an "encouragement of persecution and barbarity." Mr. Gurley says, "Should they be urged by *any stress of circumstances*, to seek an asylum beyond the limits of the United States, *humanity and religion* will alike dictate that they should be assisted to remove and establish themselves in freedom and prosperity in the land of their *choice!*" And pray, sir, is not here an allusion to the case you name on a previous page, when this same Mr. Gurley says, "Our friends at Norfolk appealed to us, and said, the people were *persecuted*, and that it was a matter of *humanity* to take them. They were *driven* from the country, and begged to go to Liberia." And yet while you thus denominate this dictate of "humanity and religion," by the names of "persecution and barbarity," you affirm, that you would have us say to the authors of these atrocities, "you shall gain nothing by your cruelty, through our instrumentality; we will not encourage your farther persecutions, by removing those whose consent you have obtained by such unjustifiable means." Truly this would be to

> "Keep the word of promise to the ear
> And break it to the hope."

Pray what would be the effect on the victims of these "barbarities," if the Colonization Society were to treat them as you recommend. Would there be either "humanity or religion," under such "*a stress of circumstances*" as those you refer to, in abandoning the poor persecuted people, and refusing to deliver them, when they "begged to go to Liberia," and invoked the humanity of their friends to appeal in their behalf. Verily, if for the purpose of rebuking these atrocities, your recommendation were adopted our "tender mercies would be cruelty."

I deplore the necessity imposed upon me, thus to bring before the reader, so flagrant evidence of " want of information," as is furnished on every page of your book but ; having undertaken this unpleasant task, I must proceed through the whole. In my next, I shall notice your 3d chapter.

With due respect,
Yours, &c.

LETTER VI.

Sir,

In your 3d chapter you direct the reader to the influence of the society upon Africa in the suppression of the slave-trade. Even Charles Stewart, the type of Garrison, and who has been imported, for the purpose of vilifying colonization, admits that the society "*interrupts* the African slave-trade within its own limits," and adds, that "the least interruption to that nefarious traffic, is an *unspeakable good !*"   But I regret to find, sir, that so far from admitting even *this* influence of colonization, you accuse the society and its members of "*ignorance, rash assertion,* and *honest confession,*" from the "astonishing medley" of which, you furnish a few choice specimens.

I have before reminded you, that the American Colonization Society is not a society for the extirpation of slavery, as you have mistaken it to be, nor is it a society for the suppression of the slave-trade, as you now insinuate; but I repeat that it is simply "a society for establishing a colony on the coast of Africa."   Nevertheless, among other collateral benefits, the *influence of the colony* in the suppression of the slave-trade, is proven by testimony, which nothing you have said can impeach.

The following extracts will show that the *intention* of the society to suppress the African slave-trade has been often declared.

"Resolved, That a committee be appointed to memorialize the Congress of the United States, requesting that they will take such further steps as to their wisdom may seem proper, to ensure the entire abolition of the African slave-trade." 3d *Report*, 1820.

"How is this trade to be abolished?   Experience teaches us that no law, no treaties stop it, though much more might be done. By laws and treaties it is already denounced, and yet

nearly 100,000 slaves are annually taken from Africa, the victims of cormorant, never-sated avarice. To suppress this trade, it must be made physically impossible. We must line the western coast of Africa with civilized settlements," &c. 14th *Report*.

Your attempt to depreciate the good done by the colony at Sierra Leone, can only be attributed to your excessive zeal against the whole scheme of colonization, for you must have known that multiplied and authentic facts are against you.

Your own excellent father expresses his opinion in a letter to Mr. Wilberforce, on the subject of the "African Institution of Great Britain, for promoting civilization and improvement in Africa." This institution, as you well know, was founded with a view to the efficiency and success of the colony at Sierra Leone, in suppressing the slave-trade. Mr. John Jay says, of this society, "It is pleasing to behold a nation assiduously cultivating the arts of peace and humanity in the midst of war, and while strenuously fighting for their all, *kindly* extending the *blessings of Christianity and civilization* to distant countries."

In Mr. Walsh's Notes of Brazil, vol. ii. p. 286, it is stated, that "from 1819 to 1828, a period of nine years, there were captured and *emancipated* by British vessels stationed at Sierra Leone, 13,821 slaves, averaging about 1400 per annum." This single fact, which you would scarcely presume to deny, speaks volumes in refutation of your attempt to deprive that colony of the merit of contributing to the suppression of the slave-trade, which, in that case, was one of the express objects for which its benevolent founders established it. That it has effected all that is desirable is not pretended by its friends, but so far as it has produced this effect, it has been an unspeakable blessing, which it is a burning shame to undervalue, much more to affirm, as you do, that it has "*actually promoted* the slave-trade!"

In turning your attention to Liberia, however, you seem to find still greater satisfaction, in an effort to convince your readers, that *no influence* whatever has been exerted on the slave-trade by that colony. Is your "want of information" again to be received as your apology. I confess, sir, that I am amazed at this portion of your book. How came you to suppress the facts which must have been known to you, of the industry, zeal, and *success*, with which the lamented Ashmun engaged in the suppression of the slave-trade in the vicinity of Liberia. Had you never read the expedition he undertook against that notorious slave-mart, Trade Town, in which three vessels were captured, 53 slaves, and subsequently 178, were liberated, and the establishment destroyed ? Had it pleased Providence to prolong his valuable life a few years longer, you would have been spared the satisfaction you seem to take, in the failure of his purpose to "banish the accursed traffic from the whole line of coast comprehended between Cape Montserado and Trade Town, both inclusive." For after announcing to the society that he had interdicted the trade from that part of the coast, he adds, " Our hopes are high that the world is to hear little or nothing more of the ravages of this detestable and outlawed traffic from this part of the coast." It is true that his sanguine hopes were not fully realized, and it is lamentable to learn that the society, after having expressed their confidence that the traffic would be utterly extinguished on the whole coast, nominally included in the colony, have not fully attained this laudable object. The colonists have done much,* and are preparing to do much more in this department, and instead of employing your pen in depreciating their efforts, it had been more in character if you had recorded a tribute to the living and the dead, for their services to the cause of humanity, memorable examples of which the history of the colony has furnished.

But I forbear to enlarge on this subject, but would simply ask you, sir, whether charity and candour did not furnish you with a better interpretation of the motives of the society and its friends, than the " ignorance, rashness, and credulousness" of which you accuse them. When the society encourage the friends of humanity by the expression of the high hopes of its friends and agents, that the slave-trade is suppressed within an hundred miles of Monrovia, and when afterward, it publishes

---

* Mr. J. F. C. Finlay, writing from Millsburg, in the colony of Liberia, to the Rev. Dr. Wilson, of Cincinnati, under date of 6th December, 1834, says,

" The colony of Liberia has done at least five times as much towards abolishing the slave-trade on this coast, as *the whole of the United States.*"

letters from its agents that the avarice and cupidity of traders, and the treachery of native kings, have again polluted the soil, by renewing the crime which they had hoped was banished from the coast, for even a greater distance ; is it fair, liberal, or just, for you to impeach their motives, and decry their well-meant endeavours ? Does not the fact that these seeming variations in their statements are published by the society itself, demonstrate their candour and veracity ? And ought not the society, after discovering that this abominable traffic yet lingers in the neighbourhood of their settlements, to stimulate the zeal and benevolence of its friends to increasing efforts for its utter extermination by publishing it to the world ? I blush that you should labour with a zeal worthy of a better cause, to deprive the society of the merit it is admitted, even by its enemies, to have earned, that of *interrupting the slave-trade.* And your attempt to disparage the character of the colonists, by impeaching them as "ignorant and depraved negroes," shows on your part a most strange incongruity with other parts of your book. They have shown thus far that they deserve better treatment, than to have it insinuated that they will not resist the "temptations of a lucrative commerce."

With due respect,
Yours, &c.

LETTER VII.

SIR,

IN your 4th chapter you assail the *missionary influence* of the colony, so determined do you seem that "no good thing shall come out of this Nazareth." And in the notice I am constrained to give to this chapter, I find the most painful part of my duty. Recognising you in the capacity of a Christian professor, I can scarcely suppress my feelings when I find such a spirit of ridicule and satire as you seem to have cultivated on this part of your subject, but still more, when I discover the monstrous extravagances and mistakes into which you have fallen. I am bound to suppose that you unfeignedly believe what you say, but I venture to predict that you will find few readers, any where, equally credulous.

Such assertions as the following are made in your book:

"They seek for the regeneration of Africa, by *emigrants who* when in the United States were denounced as a *curse and contagion* wherever they reside!"

"Of this *great company of preachers*, about 3000 of them have already set up their *tabernacle* at Liberia!"

"Pious colonizationists would, themselves, be shocked at the proposal of disgorging on the islands of the Pacific the *tenants of our prisons* under the pretext of instructing the natives in *religion and the arts,* and yet they flatter themselves, that emigrants, who, by their own showing, are less intelligent and *scarcely less guilty* than our prisoners, will by undergoing a SALT WATER BAPTISM, land in Africa wholly regenerated, and qualified as *heralds of the cross* to convert millions and millions to the faith of the gospel."

These and similar declarations can scarcely be ascribed to the "want of information," sir, for a moiety of the labour you have used in penning them, would have satisfied you that no member or friend of the Colonization Society ever entertained or expressed such preposterous anomalies as you gravely ascribe to your "fellow Christians."

It is *not true* that the regeneration of Africa was ever contemplated by means of such emigrants as you describe. It is *not true*, that "a great company of 3000 preachers" were ever supposed, by any body but yourself, to have set up their tabernacle at Liberia. It is *not true*, that the Colonization Society expect by a "salt water baptism," as you profanely assert, to convert emigrants "scarcely less guilty than our prisoners" into "*heralds of the cross.*" These, and other specimens of your unmusical and unmelodious "poetry," I repeat, are *not true.* And yet it *is true*, that "pious Christians" do regard the establishment of the colony as opening "a great and effectual door" for the preaching of that gospel which is the "power of God unto salvation," and to which *gospel* they look for the regeneration of Africa. Nor will the sneering or scoffing, either of Christians or infidels, should they be afflicted with such treatment from both these classes, at all diminish their zeal or confidence.

If you found it in your heart, sir, to treat the living among your fellow citizens and fellow Christians, with so much of contempt and satire, surely you might have spared the memory of the pious dead. Or must your "want of information" again shield you from the reproach of treating the lamented Andrews, and Bacon, and Carey, and Cox, and Cloud, and Laird, and Wright, whose ashes lie beneath the sands of Africa, with contumely and gainsaying? Do you not know that among those to whom colonizationists look for the regeneration of Africa, there are yet living missionaries of your own and other denominations, in whose behalf the whole church glorifies God, who are truly "heralds of the cross" consecrated to the work of evangelizing Africa? Are you ignorant of what every body else knows, that there are many among the emigrants who have the confidence of the whole Christian community, and whose claims to personal piety here, have been confirmed by their deportment there? And have you yet to learn that among these, there are already in the colony, ministers of the Presbyterian, Baptist, Methodist, and Episcopal churches, who are truly heralds of the cross, and that others of similar character, like Gloster,

Simpson, and Archy Moore, are even now passing through what you, in a spirit approaching to impiety, call "a salt water baptism." And are these men worthy of the "pious sneers" and profane mockery of a Christian brother? Or are those who "unfeignedly believe in the missionary influence of such, and offer contributions and prayers for the regeneration of Africa through their instrumentality," to be held up to public "odium and ridicule?" If such be the effect which anti-slavery sentiments have produced in you, sir, forgive me if I exclaim, "My soul, come not thou into their secret. To their assembly mine honour, be not thou united!"

But while you vilify the character of the colonists, ascribing to them, *en masse*, the language employed by various speakers in describing the wretchedness and depravity of multitudes of the free blacks here, and which is by them justly attributed to the neglect and oppressions they suffer in our country, and while you represent the society as sending "ship loads of vagabonds" to Africa as missionaries, in the true spirit and style of Garrisonism; I am amazed to discover that you so "*deeply regret* the attempt lately made by distinguished colonizationists to select for emigrants the *moral, industrious*, and *temperate*." And pray, let me ask the cause of this deep regret? If the "corrupt, depraved, and guilty" character of our colonists does not suit you, why should you regret that an attempt is made to "change their character in future?" "We have piped unto you, and you have not danced, we have mourned unto you, and you have not lamented." Is there no way to please you? Alas, you are concerned for our "moral rectitude," which you say is in danger, unless we "abandon colonization as a means of relieving the country from the nuisance of a free coloured population, and from the guilt and curse of slavery." Suffer me yet again to remind you, that the society does not "profess to be a remedy for slavery," nor to "remove any nuisance," but simply to establish a colony of free people of colour in Africa, with their own consent, so that your fears for our "moral rectitude" may find an object nearer home. Your reference to the Rev. Dr. Beecher, whom you accuse of "gross inconsistency, not to use a harsher term," is founded on the following resolution which the doctor offered at a meeting in Cincinnati.

" Resolved, That the establishment of colonies in Africa, by the *selection* of coloured persons, who are *moral, industrious, and temperate,* is eminently calculated to advance the cause of *civilization and religion* among the benighted native population of that continent, as well as to afford facilities to the various *missionary societies* for the prosecution of their pious designs."

This resolution, you say, is "utterly without point or meaning," thus placing under the ban of your reprobation its excellent author for the sin of colonizationism. And is there no gross inconsistency here, "not to use a harsher term?" Have you not written a chapter in condemnation of the society for *not selecting* their emigrants, and availed yourself of all the "evil speaking" that has ever been uttered against the colony for intemperance, indolence, and immorality, and now you declare a resolution to be utterly without point or meaning, which proposes in future to select the "moral, industrious, and temperate." I forbear to pain you by enlarging, let reason and conscience speak.

But you discover a still more gross inconsistency in this resolution, since you say that the *selection* proposed, is "utterly at variance with and directly opposed to the avowed *objects* of the society." And here again you repeat the old blunder, that the *objects* of the society are the abolition of slavery, which you try to prove by quoting another resolution, that they cherish the society among other reasons, because of its influence to abolish slavery. And can you make no distinction between the *influence* collaterally exerted by the society and its *objects?* I refer you again to the constitution, which may enlighten you, that you may not again repeat this day dream, by which you are yourself bewildered, and mislead your readers.

But it seems you are not content with impugning the *intelligence* of your "Christian brethren," but their *integrity* also, for you allege, that this "recent *talk* about *select* emigrants may be attributed to EXPEDIENCY." "Funds are low and temperance popular, and all at once we hear about *temperance colonies* and select emigrants." "Surely, colonizationists pay but a poor compliment to *their own candour,* or the *common sense* of the community. The truth is, there *never has been*

nor *never will be,* a selection made !"   Here then we have the
character of your "fellow Christians" drawn by yourself, and
if there be any truth in the description, "colonizationists" are
not only destitute of candour or common sense, but equally destitute of any measure of principle or veracity. I leave you to enjoy the self-complacency which are perusal of this paragraph will
afford you, and pass on, without condescending to criticise it,
for the reason that I should disdain, even to deny it.

Your last charge in this letter, is, that " the *professed* ultimate object of the society is to remove the *whole* coloured population to Africa, without any selection whatever."   Thus
you blunder on, whenever you speak of the objects of the society ; you betray the same "want of information" at every step,
and in this case, it is marvellous how you should make a quotation which disproves your own statement, in the extract from
the African Repository, where a committee of the board say that
the *free* should "be removed *as fast as their own consent can
be obtained,* and as the *means* can be found for their *removal,*
and for their *proper establishment* in Africa." Now *if* you, sir,
have faith, that the *consent* of the whole coloured population
will ever be obtained, and that the *means* will ever be found
for the removal and proper establishment of the whole in Africa, you are more credulous than any colonizationist now living.
The society, I remind you again, has no professed object but
the exclusive one contained in the second article of the constitution.

If then the system of African Colonization is, as you say,
"full of *absurdities,* and *contradictions,* and *evils,* which are
NOT SEEN, because they are concealed by a veil of prejudice,"
I fear that this veil yet obstructs your own vision, for,

> " Optics sharp it needs, I ween,
> To see what is not to be seen."

And when you think you see them, and attempt to put your
finger on them—*they are not there !*

With due respect,
Yours, &c.

LETTER VIII.

Sir,

I come now to the "Influence of the. Society on Slavery," which is the subject of your fifth chapter.

And here the reader will perceive, that you only speak of the *moral influence* expected by the friends of colonization to result from the society, and no longer urge or pretend, what you have elsewhere asserted, that it "professes to be a remedy for slavery." And yet you deny that it exerts this influence "in any degree," and after classifying the kinds of influence which must operate, you say, " it will not be pretended that the society addresses itself to the *conscience* of the slaveholder." The "want of information," not "to use a harsher term," under which you venture this ridiculous assertion, is absolutely astounding to your friends, and shows conclusively, if we had not elsewhere had cause to deplore the truth of your own sentiments, that "good men and good Christians" are led by their zeal against the society to hazard their reputation by "opinions at variance with truth and Christianity."

I would here invite your attention to the following quotations, and ask, is there no appeal to the *conscience* here?

" On the subject of slavery we must express ourselves briefly, yet *boldly*. We have heard of slavery as it exists in Asia, and Africa, and Turkey;—we have heard of the feudal slavery under which the peasantry of Europe have groaned from the days of Alaric, until now; but excepting only the horrible system of the West India Islands, we have never heard of slavery in any country, ancient or modern, Pagan, Mohammedan, or Christian, so *terrible in its character*, so *pernicious in its tendency*, so *remediless in its anticipated results*, as the slavery which exists in these United States." *Appendix to* 7th *Report*, 1824.

" The friends of human liberty are enlisting under the banner of colonization, and the advocates of perpetual despotism are arranging themselves under the banner of its adversaries, and it requires not the spirit of prophecy to foretell, whose principles in this age of *reason and religion,* and in this country of universal intelligence, will become universally popular." *Appendix to* 16th *Report,* 1833.

But Mr. Elliot Cresson is still more explicit, as may be seen by the following extract from his address: "Instead of *denouncing* an evil which they have not power to overthrow, they have recourse to the more sure but gradual mode of removing it, by enlightening the CONSCIENCES and convincing the judgments of *slaveholders.*" Were it not for your deplorable "want of information," it would be needless to inform you, that the speaker last named, has himself been instrumental in effecting the emancipation of scores, if not hundreds, of slaves. When, alas! when shall the American Anti-Slavery Society, its officers and managers, and its eulogist included, promote abolition to the extent which this single individual has done? Or, rather, when will they all cease to obstruct and hinder the cause of freedom by their angry denunciation, without effecting the emancipation of a single slave?

To prove that such appeals are not of recent date, and that *the moral influence* of the society was, from the beginning, expected to be operative in promoting emancipation, I refer you to the avowals made in the early reports.

"That they considered slavery a great *moral* and political evil, and cherished the hope and belief, that the successful prosecution of their object would offer *powerful motives* and exert a *persuasive influence* in favour of *voluntary emancipation.*" —2d *Report.*

"The hope of the gradual and *utter abolition of slavery,* in a manner consistent with the rights, interest, and happiness of society, ought *never to be abandoned.*"—*Ibid.*

And by the fourteenth report, it is shown, that the views of the society are unchanged.

"The effect of this institution, if its prosperity shall equal our wishes, will be alike propitious to every interest of our domestic society; and should it *lead*, as we may fairly hope it will, to the slow but gradual *abolition of slavery, it will wipe* from our political institutions the *only blot* which *stains* them; —and in palliation of which, we shall not be at liberty to plead *the excuse of moral necessity*, until we shall have honestly exerted *all the means* which we possess for its EXTINCTION."

"But it may be said, that the society has expressed the opinion, that slavery is a moral and political evil; and that it has regarded the scheme of colonization as presenting *motives*, and exerting a *moral* influence on the south, favourable to gradual and voluntary *emancipation*. *This is true*, and it is this, beyond all question, which has secured to it the countenance and patronage of our most profound and sagacious statesmen, and given to this scheme a peculiar attractiveness and glory in the view of the *enlightened friends of their country and of mankind*."

But a volume might be written of the proofs which the publications of the society furnish in refutation of the mistake you have here committed, in saying, that "addresses to the *conscience* are not authorized by the constitution, and are disclaimed by the society."

Hear the disinterested opinion of such men as the Rt. Rev. and venerable Bishop White, and Roberts Vaux, of Philadelphia, when they say, "We fully believe that if the society be amply sustained, it will ultimately put an end to the odious foreign traffic in human flesh, and *contribute more effectually to promote* and *insure the abolition of slavery* in the United States, than any plan that has hitherto been devised." And have we not here the testimony of those excellent men, that the *moral* influence of the colony was that to which they looked by its operation upon the *consciences* of slaveholders, for the voluntary and peaceful abolition of slavery.

But I forbear to multiply quotations, and proceed to show you, sir, that your injustice to the society is not only proven by their professions, but by their practice. The society does not merely "*promise*" to promote abolition, but exerts a mighty and successful moral influence in *actually abolishing slavery*. And here I will not refer you to the truth, which he who runs may read, that in *Kentucky, Delaware, Maryland,* and even

Virginia itself, it is now openly avowed that "*colonization doctrines have sealed the death warrant of slavery!*" Hence the pro-slavery party have declared that "colonization and emancipation are *synonimous terms,* and that the approach of the former must be *resisted!*" At a meeting of the same party in Charleston, the following toast was given, "May the infernal regions soon be *colonized* with the officers of the Colonization Society!" And while you are labouring with your misguided associates in the north, to hold up the Colonization Society, as hypocritical in its professions to exert a *moral influence* towards the voluntary and utter abolition of slavery, you are leagued with "all the advocates of the negro's perpetual bondage, who are the bitter uncompromising enemies of the ·ciety." The Rev. J. M. Danforth states on his own person. knowledge, that in South Carolina, "the society, and every thing connected with it, are held in *extreme abhorrence* by our leading men, our politicians and wealthy planters. It is so *unpopular* an institution that very few name it publicly,—it is regarded here as a *northern scheme* to *wrest* from us our *slaves.*" In your anti-colonization efforts then, you are associated in action with the very men, whose character as slaveholders is so odious, that you deprecate their connexion with the colonization cause, as an unpardonable sin. Let me conjure you, sir, no longer to be "jostled by the trafficker in human flesh," in your crusade against the society or its benevolent objects, but abandon the "bad eminence" to which your "want of information" has unhappily raised you.

Let me now invite your attention, sir, to a few *facts*, which no sophistry can evade, and until you can show a similar list, and these are only a few among many, had you not better lower your exclusive pretensions, to anti-slavery *practice,* however you may cling to a theory, which until you effect a single instance of emancipation, I must denominate in your own style to be the "baseless fabric of a vision," and call upon you in turn to give

> "To airy nothing,
> A local habitation and a name!'

The following manumissions are the legitimate result of the

" *moral influence*" of the Colonization Society, which you deny and even ridicule !

" *It would be endless to enumerate the cases of this kind that have occurred. Some of them must be recorded, that the acts and the names of the parties, where known, may have the applause to which they are entitled, and, what is of more consequence, that they may serve as stimuli to others, to follow the noble example.

" A lady, near Charleston, Va. liberated all her slaves, *ten* in number, to be sent to Liberia ; and moreover purchased *two*, whose families were among her slaves. For the one she gave $450, and for the other $350.

" The late William Fitzhugh bequeathed their freedom to *all his slaves*, after a certain fixed period, and ordered that their expenses should be paid to whatsoever place they should think proper to go. And, 'as an encouragement to them to emigrate to the American colony on the coast of Africa, where,' adds the will, ' I believe their happiness will be more permanently secured, I desire not only that the expenses of their emigration be paid, but that the sum of fifty dollars be paid to each one so emigrating, on his or her arrival in Africa.'

" David Shriver, of Frederick co. Maryland, ordered by his will, that all his slaves, *thirty* in number, should be emancipated, and that proper provision should be made for the comfortable support of the infirm and aged, and for the instruction of the young in reading, writing, and arithmetic, and in some art or trade, by which they might acquire the means of support.

" Col. Smith, an old revolutionary officer, of Sussex county, Va. ordered in his will, that all his slaves, *seventy* or *eighty* in number, should be emancipated ; and bequeathed above $5000 to defray the expense of transporting them to Liberia.

" Patsey Morris, of Louisa co., Va. directed by will, that all her slaves, *sixteen* in number, should be emancipated, and left $500 to fit them out, and defray the expense of their passage.

" The schooner Randolph, which sailed from Georgetown, South Carolina, had on board *twenty-six slaves*, liberated by a benevolent individual near Cheraw.

---

* Matthew Carey, Esq. of Philadelphia.

"Of 105 emigrants, who sailed in the brig Doris, from Baltimore and Norfolk, *sixty-two* were emancipated on condition of being conveyed to Liberia.

"Sampson David, late a member of the legislature of Tennessee, provided by will, that all his slaves, *twenty-two* in number, who are mostly young, should be liberated in 1840, or sooner, at his wife's decease, if she died before that period.

"Herbert B. Elder, of Petersburg, Va. bequeathed their freedom to all his slaves, *twenty* in number, with directions that they should be conveyed to Liberia, by the first opportunity.

"A gentleman in Georgia, has recently left *forty-nine* slaves free, on condition of their removal to Liberia.

"Mrs. Elizabeth Morris, of Bourbon co., Va. provided by will for the emancipation of her slaves, about *forty* in number.

"David Patterson, of Orange co., North Carolina, freed *eleven* slaves, to be sent to Liberia.

"Rev. Fletcher Andrew, gave freedom to *twenty*, who constituted most of his property, for the same purpose.

"Nathaniel Crenshaw, near Richmond, liberated *sixty* slaves, with a view to have them sent to Liberia.

"Rev. Robert Cox, Suffolk co., **Va.** provided by his will for the emancipation of all his slaves, upwards of *thirty*, and left several hundred dollars to pay their passage to Liberia.

"Joseph Leonard Smith, of Frederick co., Md. liberated *twelve* slaves, who sailed from Baltimore for Liberia.

"Of 107 coloured persons who sailed in the Carolinian, from Norfolk for Liberia, *forty-five* were emancipated on condition of being sent there.

"In the brig Criterion, which sailed from Norfolk for Liberia, on the 2d August, 1831, there were *forty-six* persons who had been liberated, on condition of proceeding to Liberia; 18 by Mrs. Greenfield, near Natchez; 8 by Mr. Williams, of Elizabeth city, N. C.; 7 by Gen. Jacocks, of Perquimans, Ohio; 4 by Thomas Davis, Montgomery co. Miss.; 2 by two other individuals; and 5 by some of the Quakers in North Carolina. Of those liberated slaves, 2 only were above 40 years of age, 22 were under 35, and 22 under 20.

"A gentleman in N. C., last year, gave freedom to all his slaves, 14 in number, and provided 20 dollars each, to pay their passage to Liberia.

"Mrs. J. of Mercer co., Kentucky, and her two sons, one a clergyman, and the other a physician, lately offered the Colonization Society, *sixty* slaves, to be conveyed to Liberia.

"Henry Robertson, of Hampton, Va., bequeathed their freedom to *seven* slaves, and fifty dollars to each, to aid in their removal to Liberia.

"William Fletcher, of Perquimans, N. C., ordered by will, that his slaves, *twelve* in number, should be hired out for a year after his death, to earn wherewith to pay for their conveyance to Liberia.

"A gentleman in Kentucky, lately wrote to the secretary of the society, 'I will willingly give up *twelve* or *fifteen* of my coloured people at this time; and so on *gradually*, till the whole, about *sixty*, are given up, if means for their passage can be afforded.'

"On board the Harriet, from Norfolk, of one hundred and sixty emigrants, between *forty* and *fifty* had been slaves, emancipated on condition of being sent to Africa.

"In addition to these instances, several others might be added, particularly that of Richard Bibb, Esq., of Kentucky, who proposes to send *sixty* slaves to Liberia—two gentlemen in Missouri, who desire to send *eleven* slaves—a lady in Kentucky offers *forty*—the Rev. John C. Burress, of Alabama, intends preparing *all his slaves* for colonization—the Rev. William L. Breckenridge, of Kentucky, manumitted 11 slaves, who sailed a few weeks ago from New-Orleans.

"In this work of benevolence, the Society of Friends, as in so many other cases, have nobly distinguished themselves, and assumed a prominent attitude. They have, in North Carolina, liberated no less than 652 slaves, whom they had under their care, besides, as says my authority, an unknown number of children, husbands and wives, connected with them by consanguinity, and of whom, part went to Canada, part to Liberia, part to Hayti, and a portion to Ohio. In the performance of these acts of benevolence, they expended $12,759. They had remaining under their care, in December, 1830, 402 slaves, for whom similar arrangements were to be made.

It holds out every encouragement to the Colonization Society, that the applications for the transportation of free negroes, and slaves proposed to be emancipated on condition of removal to Liberia, *far exceed its means.* There are, in North Carolina and the adjacent states, from *three to four thousand* of both descriptions, ready to embark, were the society in a situation to send them away."

The foregoing authentic *facts*, are here presented in refutation of all you have said in denial of the moral influence of colonization in *effecting* abolition and not merely promoting it. I forbear to add a single word of comment.

I pass briefly to notice the statistical calculations you make on page 74, in order to show that the scheme of transporting to Africa "the whole coloured population," is altogether impracticable. But here again you bewilder yourself and mislead your readers, by another of your "day dreams." On what authority do you assert that the object of the society is "to abolish slavery, by transporting all the free, or all the slaves, or all the annual increase?" Have you not reprobated the society because of its "single and exclusive object," and now you add another to the *many objects* you impute to it, some of which the society never dreamed of. I again remind you, sir, that the *only* object of the American Colonization Society is to *colonize*, that it will *only* colonize the *free*, and that it will *only* colonize these with *their own consent.* And *if* among the millions of slaves there shall only 3000 become free, and *if* among the free, there should only 3000 more *consent* to be colonized, then the extent of the colonization scheme will terminate with the transportation of 6000. If you then, can by your figures, tell how many of the *free*, or of those who shall become such, will *consent* to go to Africa between this time and the year 1860, the time which your calculations contemplate, you can readily satisfy yourself, that the society is guiltless of the "stupendous absurdity" of which you are the exclusive proprietor, and have earned the exclusive honour. You might have spared yourself then this Quixotic war upon a windmill of your own invention.

But you next " *assert*," in the style of dogmatizing, which I must suppose to be a recent accomplishment, acquired along with your anti-slavery creed, " that there is a *general* disposition among slaveholders to perpetuate slavery !" I am sorry, sir, that you do not feel the importance of some degree of accuracy in your assertions, and the propriety of sustaining your *ipse dixit* with some kind of evidence, especially when you contradict men whose intelligence, character, and opportunity of understanding the subject, are fully equal to your own.

Let me refer you to the speech of R. S. Finlay, Esq. at a late anniversary. He says,

" I know that much pains have been taken to *calumniate* our brethren of the south, by representing them to be the advocates of perpetual despotism. From an *extensive and familiar acquaintance* with their views and sentiments, formed upon actual observation, I know this not to be the fact. I have publicly discussed this subject *every where in the southern states*, from the eastern shore of *Maryland to the Gulf of Mexico*, in the presence of hundreds of slaves at a time, and with the general approbation of the audience to which my addresses were delivered,—and have uniformly represented it as affording the best and only safe means of *gradually* and *entirely abolishing slavery*. Indeed, so well is the moral influence of the operations of this society understood in the extreme south, that all the advocates of perpetual slavery are bitterly opposed to it, and none are its advocates, but the friends of gradual, peaceful, and ultimate *entire emancipation !*" 16th *Report*.

With such unequivocal testimony before you, how great must be the prejudice under which you " *assert* that there is a *general* disposition among slaveholders to perpetuate slavery." And how differently did a knowledge of the facts, which the history of the society furnishes, influence the venerable and immortal CLARKSON, who has devoted half a century to the cause of African emancipation. In a letter, dated Nov. 4, 1831, Mr. Clarkson says,

" For myself, I freely confess, that of all the things which have occurred in our favour since the year 1787, when the abolition of the slave trade was first seriously proposed, that which is now going on in the United States, under the auspices of the

American Colonization Society, is most important. It sur
passes any thing which has yet occurred. No sooner had the
colony been founded at Cape Montserado, than there appeared
a disposition among the owners of slaves in the United States
to give them freedom voluntarily, without one farthing of compensation, and to allow them to be sent to the land of their an-
cestors. This is to me truly astonishing! a total change of
heart in the planters, so that many thousands of slaves may be
redeemed without any cost of their redemption! Can this almost universal feeling have taken place without the interven-
tion of the Spirit of God!" .And Wilberforce, that champion
of freedom, in allusion to the same subject, and this at the time
of his high health and intellectual vigour, confessed that " warm
as his anticipations had been, they were but cold and meagre,
compared with the reality, effected by this noble plan." Such
were the voluntary tributes, paid to this society for developing
the disposition existing among slaveholders, to emancipate their
slaves, and from *British* philanthropists too. I blush, while I
exhibit them, sir, in contrast with your " *assertion ;*" while
constrained to confess that you are an American, declaring in
the face of irrefragable facts, that your own countrymen and fellow Christians are " endeavouring to transmit slavery, as a
precious inheritance to their latest posterity," and that " *no desire exists at the south to get rid of slavery.*"

I am pained at the necessity imposed upon me by duty to the
cause of truth, to meet this last statement by a palpable denial,
and the presentation of a single evidence which ought to cover
you with shame for having done so great an act of injustice. I
refer to the illustrious example of Maryland in her noble effort
to add another to the non-slaveholding states of this union.
The managers of that society avow " the *extirpation of slavery* as the *chief object* of its existence," and one " worthy of
every exertion ;" and again, "It is the DESIRE of the society that
the evil of slavery should be removed from Maryland." But
in direct contradiction to this official document, and with this sentence before you, as your quotations prove, could it have been
believed that you, sir, would " assert" that " *no desire* exists
at the south to get rid of slavery." Which are we to believe in
such a case ? Your own unsupported *assertion,* or the follow

ing preamble to their constitution, "Whereas, it is the DESIRE of the Maryland State Colonization Society, to *hasten* as far as they can the period when *slavery shall cease to exist in Maryland*," &c. I mean no disrespect when I say, that every reader will decide that you have here most grievously misrepresented the character of your fellow citizens of the south, and I forbear pursuing any farther the caricature you have drawn of this Maryland State Colonization Society, though throughout it is made up of a perversion and distortion of the facts in the case, for which I can frame no apology. You call it a "*disgraceful contrivance* to get rid of the free blacks, disguised by *insincere professions!*" "A cruel and perfidious measure." From a personal knowledge of the managers of that state society, whom you thus vilify, the most of whom are distinguished in the learned professions, and also eminent in their Christian character, I feel a righteous indignation at the hardihood which could permit you to accuse them of "disgraceful *hypocrisy, cruelty*, and *perfidy*." Where they are known, sir, you will allow me to say, without any depreciation of your station or character, even Mr. Jay will fail in staining their character, or impeaching their integrity.

I would here introduce to your notice a few brief extracts, from the writings and speeches of distinguished gentlemen in various parts of the *south* and *west*, all of whom are, or have been, extensive *slaveholders*, and I would offer these in refutation of this cruel and unjust description you give of the southern character, when you say, that "*No desire exists at the south to get rid of slavery!*" and again, "*So far from slaveholders wishing to abolish slavery, they are endeavouring to transmit it as a precious inheritance to their latest posterity;*" and "*we assert that there is a* GENERAL *disposition among slaveholders to perpetuate slavery!*" These are your assertions, made with the expressed design to convict the Colonization Society of misrepresentation and falsehood, in expressing their confidence that "there is a *growing* desire at the south to abolish slavery," and that very many slaveholders are ready to emancipate their slaves, so soon as the society provides the means for their emigration. The following brief extracts will amply refute your statements, and sustain those of the Colonization Society. You will not question that the speakers are as respectable and credible as yourself.

Patrick Henry.

"I repeat it again, that it would rejoice my very soul that *every one* of my fellow beings was *emancipated*. As we ought with gratitude to admire that decree of heaven which has numbered us among the *free*, we ought to *lament and deplore* the necessity of holding our fellow men in bondage."—*Debates in Virginia Convention.*

Zachariah Johnson.

"Slavery has been the foundation of that impiety and dissipation which have been so much disseminated among our countrymen. If it were *totally abolished*, it would do much good." *Ibid.*

Judge Tucker.

"The introduction of slavery into this country, is, at this day,* considered among its *greatest misfortunes.*" And in 1803, he said, after pronouncing slavery to be "a calamity, a reproach, and a curse,"—"those who wish to postpone emancipation, do not reflect that every day renders the task more arduous to be performed."

General Harper.

'It tends, and may powerfully tend, to rid us gradually and entirely in the United States, of slaves and slavery, a great moral and political evil, of increasing virulence and extent, from which much mischief is now felt, and very great calamity in future, is justly apprehended. It speaks not only to our understandings, but to our senses; and however it may be derided by some, or overlooked by others, who have not the ability or time, or do not give themselves the trouble to reflect on, and estimate properly, the force and extent of those great moral and physical causes, which prepare gradually, and at length bring forth the most terrible convulsions in civil society; it will not be viewed without deep and awful apprehensions by any who shall bring sound minds, and some share of political knowledge and sagacity, to the serious consideration of the subject. Such persons will give their most serious attention to

---

* This was said as early as 1795.

any proposition whicn has for its object, the eradication of this terrible mischief lurking in our vitals."—*Letter on Coloniza-tion Society.*

Darby.

" Copying from Montesquieu, and not from observation of na-ture, climate has been called upon to account for stains on the human character, imprinted by the hand of political mistake. No country where negro slavery is established, but must bear, in part, the wounds inflicted on nature and justice. Without pursuing a train of metaphysical reasoning, we may at once draw this induction, that if slavery, like pain, is one of the laws of existence, the latter does not more certainly produce physical weakness, debility, and death, than does the former lessen the purity of virtue in the human breast."—*History of Louisiana.*

M'Call.

" It is shocking to human nature, that any race of mankind, and their posterity, should be sentenced to perpetual slavery." *History of Georgia.*

General Mercer.

" For, although it is believed, and is, indeed, too obvious to require proof, that the colonization of the free people of colour alone, would not only tend to civilize Africa; to abolish the slave-trade; and greatly to advance their own happiness; but to promote that also of the other classes of society, the proprietors and slaves; yet the hope of the gradual and utter abolition of slavery, in a manner consistent with the rights, interests, and happiness of society, ought never to be abandoned."—*Report to Colonization Society.*

F. S. Key, Esq.

" I hope I may be excused, if I add, that the subject which engages us, is one in which it is our right to act—as much our right to act, as it is the right of those who differ from us not to act. If we believe in the existence of a great moral and po-litical evil amongst us, and that duty, honour, and interest, call upon us to prepare the way for its removal, we must act. All that can be required of us, is, that we act discreetly," &c. *Speech before Colonization Society.*

Mr. Clay.

" If they would repress all tendencies towards liberty and ultimate emancipation, they must do more than put down the benevolent efforts of this society. They must penetrate the human soul, and eradicate the light of reason, and the love of liberty. Our friends, who are cursed with this *greatest of human evils*, (slavery,) deserve our kindest attention and consideration. Their property and safety are both involved."— *Speech before Colonization Society.*

William H. Fitzhugh, Esq.

"Slavery, in its mildest form, is an evil of the darkest character. Cruel and unnatural in its origin, no plea can be urged in justification of its continuance, but the plea of necessity; not that necessity which arises from our habits, our prejudices, or our wants; but the necessity which requires us to submit to existing evils, rather than substitute, by their removal, others of a more serious and destructive character. There is no riveted attachment to slavery, prevailing extensively, in any portion of our country. Its injurious effects on our habits, our morals, our individual wealth, and more especially on our national strength and prosperity, are universally felt, and almost universally acknowledged."

Mr. Levasseur.

"Happily, there is no part of the civilized world, in which it is necessary to discuss the justice or injustice of the principle of negro slavery; at the present day, every sane man agrees that it is a monstrosity, and it would be altogether inaccurate, to suppose that there are in the United States, more than elsewhere, individuals sufficiently senseless to seek to defend it, either by their writings or conversation. For myself, who have traversed the twenty-four states of the union, and in the course of a year have had more than one opportunity of hearing long and keen discussions upon this subject, I declare that I never have found but a single person, who seriously defended this principle. This was a young man, whose head, sufficiently imperfect in its organization, was filled with confused and ridiculous notions relative to Roman History; and appeared to be completely ignorant of the history of his own country. It would be waste of time, to repeat here, his crude and ignorant tirade."

Now, sir, if the sentiments of these men of eminent talents, citizens of the south, and slaveholders, do not convict you of having caricatured and calumniated the southern character, surely you will retract this act of cruelty and injustice, when you read the following extracts from "the Southern Review," which is the acknowledged representative of the slaveholding region, and expresses itself thus while vindicating the present necessity of the system, though deprecating its perpetuity.

"The *conscientious* slaveholder deserves a larger share of the sympathy of those who have sympathy to spare, than any other class of men, not excepting the slave himself." "One *great evil* of the system is its tendency to produce disorder and poverty in a country." "The slave-trade may be regarded as a *conspiracy* of all Europe and the commercial part of this continent, not only against Africa, but in a *more aggravated sense, against these southern regions.*"

But if all this were insufficient, let me add the testimony of that same Mr. Harrison, of Virginia, whose language you have so perverted, and "vilified," in another part of your book. He says, speaking from personal knowledge, to which you cannot pretend,

" Almost all masters, in Virginia, assent to the proposition, that when slaves can be liberated without *danger to themselves,* and to their *own* advantage, it ought to be done. If there are few who think otherwise in Virginia, I feel assured that *there are few such any where in the south!*"

Surely you cannot suppose that such vituperation and censoriousness as you have here indulged, against this Maryland scheme, and the entire south, can produce conviction in any mind, or commend your "inquiry" to the candid and intelligent. Nor can you so far deceive yourself as to suppose that "this is the style *to do good with.*" It is plain that your zeal in behalf of anti-colonizationism has "eaten you up," and reason, conscience, and *religion* itself, are all powerless in restraining your wrath.

With due respect,
Yours, &c.

LETTER IX.

SIR,

HAVING deceived yourself into the belief that the Colonization Society is *impotent*, and the scheme is *impracticable*, you next call on " the friends of humanity and religion to meet it with *unrelenting hostility*, to labour *without rest* and *without weariness* for its *entire prostration*." When you began your book you called it a " *powerful institution*," and now you proclaim its " *utter impotency*," which you explain by saying it is " powerless for good, but *mighty for evil*." And having set the example of " *unrelenting hostility*," you invoke "humanity and religion," and the friends of both, to enlist under your banner, on which is inscribed,

" The extinction of the American Colonization Society, the first step to the abolition of slavery !"

Here, then, is the attitude you assume, and rally the forces of " immediate abolitionism" by this war-cry. Be it so. Let it be distinctly understood that " we are not the attacking party ;—the American Colonization Society does not make war upon any man or any association of men. With the American Anti-Slavery Society we have nothing to do, further than in self-defence ; and meanwhile we rejoice, and will rejoice, in contemplating any measure of good which may be effected by all other societies, for the African race."

In the recapitulation of the allegations against the society, which you introduce into this long chapter, you repeat that it " *professes* to be a remedy for slavery, and the only one," a charge which I have shown in a former letter to be without any foundation in truth. And you exhibit your own melancholy inconsistency, by attempting to convict the society's publications of contradictions, in having insisted that the *object* of the society is *not* emancipation, while its *moral influence* in promo-

ting that cause, is so often referred to, thus refusing to acknowledge the obvious distinction between the single and exclusive
object of the society, and those collateral benefits which its
friends expect from its success. Such disingenuousness and
uncandid fault-finding I have had frequent occasion to rebuke,
in previous parts of this correspondence, and shall not dwell on
it here.

The following is, however, a distinct retraction of most of
the charges I have refuted, and presents your opposition in
another form.

" We fully admit that the society has no more right to *meddle with emancipation or slavery*, than a Bible society ;—
and we condemn it, because disregarding its *professed object*,
and in utter contempt of its own *constitution*, it has lent itself
to *support and perpetuate* a system of *cruelty* and *wickedness*."
" We will now proceed to show that the society has stepped out
of its sphere to acknowledge that man may have *property in
man*, to *justify* him for holding this property, and to *vilify* all
who would *persuade* him instantly to surrender it."

There are here three distinct and explicit accusations, each of
which is denied. I will now consider them separately :

1st. The society " *acknowledges* that man may have property in man."

This you attempt to sustain by quotations from the African
Repository, in which the " *rights* of the slaveholders are *respected as sacred*." Now any schoolboy (pardon the allusion)
will perceive that the *rights* here acknowledged as sacred, are the
legal rights of the slaveholder, and not the abstract rights, for
which some contend. Hence, the respect is shown to the " law
of the land," and does not imply, as is falsely insinuated, the
justification of those laws. So far from this, the society thus
expresses itself, in the face of heaven and earth, " That slavery
is a *moral and political evil*, is a truth inscribed, as it were,
upon the firmament of heaven, the face of the earth, and the
heart of man ;—the denial of which would be the denial of the
fundamental principle of all free governments."

2d. You next accuse the society of " *excusing and justifying* slaveholders." This charge comes with a singular grace, from one who blames the society for "*professing* to be a *remedy* for slavery, and being about to *abolish* it," and especially in the face of the fact, that those in the south who do " *excuse and justify*" the system, regard it as a "northern device to wrest from them their slaves." But could you, sir, expect that the sanction of your name would establish this allegation, coupled as it is with a form of prayer to be used by the head of a family, in the slave region, published by the excellent Bishop Meade, himself a zealous colonizationist ?

"O heavenly Master, hear me while I lift up my heart in prayer, for those unfortunate beings who *call me master*. O God make known to me my *whole duty* towards them and their oppressed race, and give me courage and zeal to do it *at all events*. Convince me of *sin*, if I be *wrong* in retaining them *another moment* in bondage."

Is there any thing here like excusing or justifying slaveholding. And if Bishop Meade, himself a zealous colonizationist, recommends this prayer to the pious colonizationists who are slaveholders in the south, and who daily use this "manual of devotion," how then do you say that "conscience and the word of God, death, judgment, and eternity, enter not into the composition of colonization," and that the society "disclaims all appeals to the conscience," p. 73.

3d. But you affirm, lastly, that "the society *vilifies* all who would *persuade* the slaveholder instantly to emancipate." I shall not examine the evidence you bring to bolster up this assertion, in detail, in this letter, but would here only record my unqualified denial even of its semblance of truth. The society *vilifies* nobody, nor do you furnish a particle of testimony in proof of any vilification, though your own book "vilifies" that society in the worst sense of that term, as I have already shown. But the opinions expressed by the society and its friends, against anti-slavery societies, every reader will perceive is in no instance against "*persuading* slaveholders to emancipate," as you most unjustly allege. And though the society cannot as such interfere with the subject of slavery, because of its single and exclusive object, yet tens of thousands of its members, including very many slaveholders, would unite with those who would

"*persuade* masters to emancipate;" and IF this were the profession and practice of the anti-slavery societies, the Colonization Society would rejoice to welcome them as auxiliaries in
their benevolent designs, and its members would every where
exclaim, "Let there be no strife I pray thee, between me
and thee, between my herdsmen and thy herdsmen, for we be
brethren."

It is not true, then, that the society vilifies those who would
persuade slaveholders to emancipate, though it is conceded, that
similar unkind and unfounded attacks, to that which you have
made, have led some of its friends to "err from their propriety,"
and may have led the society, in its own vindication, sometimes
in language, to violate its strict neutrality.   For, in the language
of Gerrit Smith, the able advocate of emancipation, and the true
friend of the Colonization Society, "Such is, or should be the
neutrality of our society, that its members may be free on the
one hand to be slaveholders, and on the other to join the Anti-
Slavery Society, without doing violence to their connexion with
the Colonization Society."   For there are thousands of us, and
God is my record, I am one of them, who "joined the Colonization Society in the spirit, and with the objects of abolitionists.
In that spirit, and with these objects, we continue our connexion
with it."

You need not marvel then, sir, if men who have some share
of reputation and intelligence, however inferior in either to
yourself, should, when assailed with misrepresentation, ridicule,
opprobrium, and abuse, sometimes write and speak unadvised-
ly, and even unguardedly, in temper I mean, in self-vindication.   A conscientious integrity may sustain a man under any
measure of persecution for righteousness' sake, but when his
motives are impugned, his principles impeached, his opinions
and practice perverted, and his claims to Christianity itself,
denied, it is a duty he owes to the cause of truth, that he enter
his disclaimer, record his protest, and prove his innocence.   To
be sure he should do this as a Christian, "not rendering railing
for railing, but contrariwise;" nevertheless, he is not responsible
for the wounds which his adversary may receive from *his own
darts*, when their points are made to recoil upon himself.

And here, sir, I would briefly refer to the proofs you present, with your assertion, that the society is in fact an

Anti-Abolition Society.

The extract from the speech of a Mr. Harrison, of Virginia, is that on which your chief reliance is placed, and which, as I shall show, you not only pervert, but of which you make an illogical and illegitimate use. And first, I would remind you, that at the time that speech was delivered, it was in vindication of the society from formidable opposition, originating in the south, among the *advocates of slavery*, then more numerous than now. They had sought to prejudice the friends of the cause against the Colonization Society, by denying its professed neutrality on the subject of slavery, and attributing a secret design of promoting *abolition*, calling it a "northern device to wrest from us our slaves." For notwithstanding the constitutional declaration of our single and exclusive object, yet the practical moral influence of the society's operations had thus early resulted in so many instances of *voluntary emancipation*, that the pro-slavery party had become alarmed. It was in this state of things, that Mr. Harrison disclaimed alliance with "any *abolition* society in America or elsewhere," and added, that the society was "ready, when there is need, to *pass a censure* upon such societies in America." This language, which, in one of your rhetorical flourishes, you call an "unblushing outrage," was intended and understood at the time, to be nothing more than the strongest possible assurance, that the charge of sinister or secret designs to exert any direct action upon slavery,— would be a violation of our professions, and was utterly false. It was saying to the advocates of perpetual slavery, if you continue to repeat your calumny, until "there is need," we shall not barely disclaim our alliance with abolition societies of which you accuse us, but will, by a public act, "pass a censure upon such societies," and thus brand you with this evidence of falsehood. Where then, sir, is that charity which "thinketh no evil," and which "puts the most favourable construction even on the most unfavourable appearances," in the strange perversion of this sentiment into an "unblushing outrage."

But the use you make of it, is still worse than its perversion, for you apply the proposed censure to the "abolition societies," founded by the influence of such men as Franklin, and your distinguished father, and other illustrious citizens, who advocated *gradual* abolition. And it is against these that you allege that the society was ready to "pass a censure." But is not this obviously a wild conceit of your morbid imagination? These societies had existed more than forty years before, and more than thirty years when the Colonization Society was formed; and yet, though they were worthy of all praise, in doing all that their scheme was capable of effecting, yet the "scattered and feeble rays of light," as you admit, had scarcely "begun to pierce the dense cloud which brooded over the southern country," and hence no alarm or resistance was felt among the advocates for slavery, nor would their plan have ever roused the fears of the pro-slavery party. During forty years their scheme of *gradual* abolition had not sensibly affected the slaveholding states, but in 1828, the Colonization Society had made such an impression, and produced voluntary abolition in so many instances, that fears were entertained that this new scheme of *gradualism* was becoming too much like *immediatism*, and *now* the friends of perpetual slavery, began to tremble. Now the abolition societies, before regarded as harmless things, became an object of dread, and fears were expressed that they might be made powerful engines in the hands of the Colonization Society, to do what their own constitution prohibited them from doing by direct action. And hence it became necessary, in the opinion of Mr. Harrison, to disclaim "alliance" with them, and promise, "if need be, to pass a censure upon them." This mode of concession, is often the most powerful form of rhetoric, and at the time was not without its effect upon the pro-slavery enemies of colonization. But it is the essence of absurdity to suppose that he had any unfriendly design or tendency upon the abolition societies; for at that time, 1828, many of the prominent friends of these societies, were *actively enlisted* in the cause of colonization, a circumstance which probably first awakened the jealousy of southern men, which Mr. Harrison thought it proper to remove, by the language he used.

But you have persuaded yourself, that this *promised censure,*

—promised "when there is need," and *never performed*, because never needed, has had the effect of "withering and shrinking" the "abolition societies and their conventions !" How strange the infatuation which could attribute such mighty results to such an inefficient cause ! Surely, Mr. Harrison little thought when he made that speech, such stupendous consequences would follow, and better had it have been for him if you had never enlightened him by this discovery, for in such a case truly,

"Ignorance were bliss, and it were folly to be wise."

Still, however, you have made a more extraordinary use of this speech than either of those I have named, for you not only scandalously deteriorate the character of the old abolition societies by attempting to make it appear that the new anti-slavery societies, are their legitimate successors, but even call them "*more* sturdy associations." Spirit of Franklin, Jay, and Benezet ! Look on *this* picture and then on *that !* Your language is,

"Within the last two years, the abolition societies have been partially *succeeded* by *more sturdy* associations, named *Anti-slavery Societies*, which, instead of quailing beneath the *frowns* of their FOE ! have dared to grapple with him in mortal conflict, and to stake the hopes of freedom on the issue."

In the name of the abolition societies alluded to, sir, I protest against their incongruous association in any aspect with the anti-slavery societies, much less as inferior to them; I regard it as worse than "amalgamation of colours."*

---

* Notwithstanding Mr. Jay so spiritedly repels the charge against modern abolitionists, of desiring amalgamation, as a calumny, and declares that "he must be deeply imbued with fanaticism, or rather insanity," who contends for the "reception in our families, and a place at our tables" for the blacks; yet the following significant hint, at *another kind of amalgamation*, is given by himself, on his 28th page, where he affirms :—
"It is not very *reputable* to our republicanism and religion, that there should be *any necessity* for seminaries for the *exclusive* use of such of our fellow countrymen as *happen* to have *darker complexions* than our own." Let me recommend, that in the promised *second edition*, either this sentence should be omitted, or the disclaimer alluded to, for both will hardly find credit.

I deny that the former ever "*quailed*" before any "*frowns*," or that the Colonization Society ever was their "*foe*." And as to the "daring to mortal conflict" of which you speak, I greatly rejoice to know that the "hopes of freedom" are not in the keeping of your Anti-Slavery Societies, and that they cannot therefore "stake them on any issue." No, sir, the "hopes of freedom" will be consummated, if both our society and your "sturdy associations" were annihilated to-morrow; for they who oppose, must "gird themselves for warfare against all the friends of virtue and of liberty, of man and of God."

Believe me, sir, you deceive yourself egregiously, when you suppose that the freedom and "happiness of millions depends on *your* efforts," or those of what you are pleased to call your "haughty adversary," the Colonization Society. But if they did, you should remember, that "the end does not always sanctify the means."

With due respect,
Yours, &c.

LETTER X.

SIR,

As an evidence of the character and tendency of the abolition societies, to which so frequent reference is made, and in proof also, that Col. Wm. L. Stone has, for a great many years, exhibited a consistency of character, which ought to shield him from the obloquy and reproach you have so profusely poured upon him in your book, I would remind you of the Anti-Slavery Convention, held at Baltimore, in 1826, by the Abolition Manumission Societies, and the prominent part Mr. Stone took in the proceedings of the Convention. The following preamble and resolutions, among others, which that calumniated man then proposed for the adoption of that body, demonstrate that he felt and acted, *nine years ago*, as an abolitionist, which he still continues to be in the Colonization Society.

" Whereas it is represented by the *great body* of the *owners of slaves*, that slavery is a *grievous evil*, and its continuance and increase fraught with many appalling dangers :—and whereas, the friends of emancipation are frequently called upon by the proprietors of slaves, to devise some adequate means to rid the country, by *a safe and gradual process*, of a population whose continuance amongst us is so *unnatural*, and whose rapid multiplication is so *alarming ;*—and whereas many of the northern states have assisted, in former times, to entail this *curse* upon the land, by countenancing slavery themselves, and allowing their citizens to participate in the African slave-trade : and whereas, the safety, prosperity, and happiness, of any one portion of these United States, is *alike dear to all ;*—and whereas, in the opinion of this convention, it is expedient for the nation to put forth its strength in a concentrated effort, to *free this happy country* from so great a calamity, without a forcible interference with *rights of property, sanctioned indirectly*, at least, by the constitution, therefore,

"Resolved, That the Congress of the United States be requested to commence the great work of *emancipation* by *immediately abolishing slavery, within* THE DISTRICT OF COLUMBIA, and causing the persons set at liberty to be transported to Hayti, or to the *western coast of Africa;* or either, which they may *choose* for a residence.

"And whereas, in the opinion of this convention, as a general rule, ignorance and vice are inseparable companions, and the best way to make good servants, is to *enlighten their understandings,* and *improve their hearts,* by wholesome, moral, and religious instruction; and whereas, it is admitted on all hands, that sooner or later the *work of emancipation must be undertaken, and prosecuted to its completion;* Therefore, in order that the slaves may be better fitted to appreciate and enjoy the blessings of freedom—

"Resolved, That it be recommended by this convention to the legislatures of the several states, where personal slavery exists, to *repeal all laws* in any manner prohibiting the moral and religious instruction of the slaves.

"Resolved, That the proprietors of slaves in the United States be respectfully requested by this convention, to encourage, *by all possible means,* the *instruction of their slaves in reading,* and the rudiments of a common English education, together with the leading doctrines of Christianity, by *Sunday Schools,* and such other means as may be within their power!"

Such were the sentiments of this " distinguished colonizationist," in 1826, and then equally distinguished in the " Abolition Societies," for there was, and is, *no uncongeniality,* as these resolutions prove : and most of them were adopted by the convention, composed of delegates, from many of the states of this union, appointed by the *Abolition Societies.* This will still be more apparent by the following resolution, which was *adopted* by the convention.

"Resolved, That this convention would approve of an adequate appropriation of the public revenue of the United States, for the *voluntary removal* of such slaves, as may hereafter be *emancipated,* to any country, which they may select for their future residence."

Here, then, we have the voice of the assembled wisdom, and

philanthropy, of those Manumission and Abolition Societies, of the first of which, your venerable father was the president. And let me ask you, sir, how you could persuade yourself, to repre-sent the present Anti-slavery Society, as a *kindred* institution, after reading the foregoing preamble, and the several resolutions, I have adduced ; much less insinuate, as you do, that it is a successor in the same objects ? And pray, sir, with these "authentic facts," known to you, let me inquire, with what consistency, or semblance of truth, do you affirm, that "the Colonization Society *vindicates the cruel laws*, which are crushing these people to the dust," and present a " *unanimous*, vigorous, and persevering *opposition*, to present manumission," and that, "NO MEMBER of the Colonization Society has, hitherto, been rash enough to make the attempt, to recommend the free blacks to the *sympathy of Christians*, to propose SCHOOLS for their instruction, plans for encouraging their industry, and *efforts for their moral and religious improvement?*" I need not tell you, that Colonel Stone was a member of the Colonization Society, in 1826,* when, in a convention of abolitionists, he thus "made the attempt," "proposed schools," and other " efforts for the moral and religious improvement of these people," and presented a powerful appeal against those " cruel laws," which you charge the whole of us with " *vindicating !*" Your candid confession, of " want of information," is the *only* reparation which can ever atone, for this outrage upon individual character, as well as upon that noble institution, the Colonization Society, which you so unjustly assail.

From the report of Mr. Stone's speech, before the convention at Baltimore, the following extract is worthy of preservation, and is affectionately commended to your candour and intelligence, with the single remark, that it expresses the feelings and views of the great body of colonizationists, whom you vilify, and is strictly in conformity with the sentiments of the society, which you so strangely misrepresent. It is appended

---

* He wrote a vindication of the Colonization Society, so long ago as 1819, and though he wavered for a time, by reason of the delusive hopes of the Haytien project, yet he continues still, with thousands of us, to advocate colonization, *because he is an abolitionist.*

to an argument, in favour of a scheme of "*emancipation* and *colonization*," under the patronage of the general government.

"In undertaking a work of this magnitude, *compromises* will be found as necessary as they were in forming the federal compact. We must take men as they are, and things as they are. And we must move in this business with a FULL CONVICTION, that the *slaveholders* and *slave states* must *act with us*, in this matter. *They* must give *their consent* to the emancipation of their slaves, and *we* must offer the *inducements*. It will not do, therefore, to *refine* too much. And although we *do not believe it lawful, in the sight of heaven*, to hold flesh and blood as *property*, still we must, from motives of expediency, *act as though it were so*. We have no disposition to interfere with the rights of property, nor with the subsisting relations between master and slave. We would not liberate the slaves *en masse*, in their present condition, and let them loose upon this community, but would transport them, with their own consent, if possible, or prepare them to enjoy the blessings of freedom in some part of our own country. We have not come to the south, to scatter firebrands, arrows, and death, but to meet our southern friends on neutral ground, and *join* them in a mighty effort to rid them of an evil which they all affect to deplore."

With the foregoing reference to abolition societies, and extracts from the language of a "leading colonizationist," I leave them, and him, to the judgment and candour of the reader, who may form his own opinion, of your attempt to identify the former with the anti-slavery societies, or impute to the latter, the destitution of principle of which you accuse him.

After vainly attempting to identify yourself and your associates with the former "abolition societies," you inadvertently refute yourself by admitting that they were for "*gradual* abolition," while you utterly repudiate all gradualism. I shall, therefore, waive all farther reference to this topic at present, and proceed to notice your complaints that the "*rights*" of abolitionists have been invaded by colonizationists. And as among the first and most formidable in your list of grievances, you have placed Colonel W. L. Stone, editor of the Commercial Advertiser, and very frequently in your book aluded to him, and his press I shall here allow him to speak

for himself in reference to the most prominent of the charges
you so unjustly make against him. I deem this course due to
that estimable man, whom I regard as a fellow Christian, and
especially because the Commercial Advertiser, he conducts, is so
valuable an auxiliary to every good work, that its vindication
is a subject in which the cause of public morals is largely involved. I extract the following from the Commercial Advertiser, of March 24th, 1835.

" Truly we have fallen upon evil times and evil days. Never
did we expect to meet with *such* a book, from the pen of the
son and biographer of the illustrious John Jay. And *such* a
son !—a man of high political and moral worth—of scholarship,
and sound integrity. But fanaticism is a contagion, which
sometimes seizes upon the gifted and the good, as well as upon
the weak brother, and the bolder hypocrite. Of this truth, we
have a melancholy instance before us—affording another example of the exceeding virulence of this last species of fanaticism, which, like the cholera among diseases, exceeds in malig-
nant power all that have gone before it. Why it should be so,
we know not: but it seems to be the fact, that wherever, and
upon whomsoever, this spirit of immediate and unconditional
abolitionism fastens itself, it drives reason from her empire;
divests Christianity of all her sweetest charities and graces;
sears the conscience as with a hot iron; and tramples the Divine
attribute of Truth under foot. Mr. Jay has selected for his
motto, the following passage from Milton:—' Give me the
liberty to know, to utter, and to argue freely, according to my
conscience, above all liberties.' The sentiment is good as far
as it goes; but before we shall have completed the present article, the reader will have reason to regret that the author had
not governed himself by another maxim, to be found likewise
in an English poet, yet older than Milton, and equally illustrious.

> . . " ' In thy right hand carry gentle peace.
> . . . . . . Be just, and fear not :
> Let all the ends thou aim'st at, be thy country's,
> Thy God's, and Truth's; then if thou fall'st,
> Thou fall'st a blessed martyr.'

"Had the author selected such a motto, and written in its spirit, we should have been spared the pain of writing the present article,—which, from the high regard we have ever entertained for Mr. Jay, and the affection we cherish for him still, notwithstanding the cruel misrepresentations by which we are assailed in the volume before us, renders its composition one of the most unpleasant acts of editorial duty we have for many years been called upon to discharge.

"A highly valued clerical friend admonished us the other day, that the immediate abolitionists in this city were engaged in a desperate effort to fasten the responsibility of the abolition riots of last summer, upon the Commercial Advertiser, and the writer of this article in particular ; and he advised us to be pre-pared for an attack, (from a quarter least expected,) which it would be necessary for us to meet with firmness and decision. The caution was given in relation to the work now before us.

"But the information as to the existence of the foul design respecting the riots, was not new.   It is an effort in which both the tongues and the pens of the immediate abolitionists have been engaged, with an energy and a zeal worthy of a better cause, ever since *they themselves, by their own publications, and their own acts, spoke those riots into existence, and had well nigh perished in the flames of their own kindling*.   And it is in furtherance of this design, that the author has been induced by evil counsellors, to put forth the volume before us, and in which it is melancholy to find, that such a man as WILLIAM JAY should appear, not only in alliance with the notorious Garrison, but as his apologist—nay, his eulogist ! Equally painful, also, and greatly amazing, will it be to the friends of Mr. Jay, to find his name in the title of a book, consisting, in a great measure, of the unfair and garbled extracts from the publications of the Colonization Society, and of others friendly to it, or perhaps connected with it, which have for a few years past graced the columns of the New-York Evangelist, and such scandalous journals, as Garrison's Liberator, and the Emancipator.   And yet such is the fact.   The Hon. William Jay, strange as it may appear, has been persuaded—it needs no familiar to tell by what coterie of *pseudo philanthropists*—to lend his name to such a compilation—accompanying it with remarks conceived in the same spirit of candour, which **first** prompted the system of garbled quotations, for the purpose of charging upon the Colonization Society and its friends, the maintenance of doctrines, opinions, and designs, which they have not only never entertained, but have uniformly and most emphatically repudiated.

" The practice of these abolitionists in this matter, has been upon precisely the same principle that the Atheist proves from the Bible that *' there is no God,'* viz. : by omitting the antecedent and most important portion of the sentence—*' The fool hath said in his heart.'* It is exactly after that manner, that this journal has been treated by the abolitionists in regard to the riots of last summer. For instance, when in common with a vast majority of the most respectable people in this city, we saw to what the perverse counsels of the immediate abolitionists were leading, we should have been recreant to our duty, had we not remonstrated. After Garrison's shameful calumnies upon his own country in Europe—uttered, too, in the presence of such men as Anson G. Phelps, and Thomas A. Ronalds, of this city, it was easy to foresee that his presence here, to form a society in furtherance of his wretched theories, would inevitably lead to tumult. The abolitionists were told as much—though not in this paper, however, as has been falsely asserted. But they persisted in their course ; and the result was such as might have been anticipated, and in some respects, as all good men deplored. Nor did they learn wisdom from experience ; but from that day, until the disgraceful riots of July, the course of these misguided people was the same, or rather, it was marked, from day to day, with increasing folly. The scenes of May, in the Chatham-street Chapel, will not soon be forgotten. It was in vain that we protested, over and over again, against such transactions, and admonished the leaders of the consequences in which they would result, and which, in a community so highly and wickedly exasperated, no wisdom nor forecast would be able to prevent.

" The public and ostentatious examination of the worthless instrument, Brown, and the loathsome questions which the managers of that wretched, but insulting farce, put to him, awakened a storm of popular indignation which could scarcely then be controlled.   Afterwards followed the inflammatory lectures in the chapel ; and in connexion therewith, a notice of a fouth of July celebration of the fanaticism, to be held at the same place.   It occurred to us at once, and not to us only, that *such* a celebration, on *such* an occasion, when all the elements of popular violence would be in motion, would be an exceedingly hazardous experiment, and we deemed it a duty to write and publish a temperate remonstrance against the procedure.   But as before without effect.   The result is known.

" Now we do not pretend to say, that the leaders of the abolitionists actually designed to bring about those riots.   We do not believe they did.   But their object was indisputably to produce a strong degree of excitement ; and they succeeded, by means of their meetings, their inflammatory newspapers, and their incendiary handbills, written by one of the principal officers of their society, in effecting a higher degree of excitement than they intended.   Still, we concede, that they did not really mean to stimulate to riot ; but we are free to say, at the same time, that if it were our design now, to kindle another series of riots, we should, as the most certain method, pursue exactly the course which they then pursued.   But against all these things we remonstrated ; and because we did so, and the results corresponded with our predictions, the authors of the incendiary publications, and the Chatham-street scenes, which, beyond all doubt, caused the riots, turned short about, and have from that day to the present made the country ring with charges against us, of creating riots fomented by themselves, and against the measures leading to which we were solemnly imploring and protesting.

" We now come to the book itself, of which the reader will already have formed some idea from what is said, and truly said, above.   The volume is, from beginning to end, a continued attack upon the Colonization Society and its friends— filled with acrimonious and illiberal allegations against that noble institution, which the author obviously perceives to be the ' great mountain' in the way of the visionary schemes in which he has embarked ; and, as we have already intimated, we are sorry to say that he repeats and endorses all the stereotyped calumnies of the Garrison tribe of scribblers, though so often disclaimed and refuted.   And in this crusade against the society, standing in the relation to it which we have done for years past, it was hardly to have been expected that we should escape at least a passing notice.

"In common with many others, therefore, abler and better than ourselves, the writer of this article has been selected by name, for vindictive reprobation.   But we do not murmur at the distinction of being thus included in the same denunciation with the great and good men of this land—many of whom are named in terms which could hardly have been expected from the author—a circumstance which can only be accounted for by the bewildering mental and moral association to which he now belongs.   We have no room to go into any detailed re-futation of the gross misrepresentations of fact and of senti-ment, to be found in this book, and must content ourselves with a single example—an example, however, which will fall with withering effect upon the work of which it is a specimen.   We quote the following passage:

"'The abolitionists in New-York gave notice of a meeting for forming a City Anti-Slavery Society.   In reference to this notice, the chairman of the executive committee of the New-York Colonization Society, Mr. Stone, published in his paper, 2d October, 1833, the following:

"'Is it possible, that our citizens can look quietly on, while the flames of discord are rising? while even our pulpits are sought to be used for the base PURPOSE of encouraging scenes of *bloodshed* in our land.   If we do, can we look our southern brethren in the face, and say, we are opposed to interfering with their rights?   No, we cannot.

"'The HINT thus kindly given, was readily taken, and a mob of 5000 scattered the abolitionists.'—*Jay's Inquiry*, pp. 110, 111.

"Now, what is the inference which the unsophisticated reader will draw from this extract?   And what was the inference which the author *intended* his readers should draw from it? Does he not mean, by the use of a little adroit phraseology, to charge upon us the passage which he has quoted from the Commercial of October 2d, 1833, as an editorial article, sanctioned by an officer of the Colonization Society, as such?   Does he not, moreover, intend to be understood as charging this publication upon Mr. Stone, with the express design of creating a riot? It cannot be otherwise.   The public will understand him as meaning to impute alike the sentiment, the authorship, and the base design of creating a riot, to Mr. Stone. 'The *hint*, thus *kindly given*, &c. Does not Mr. Jay mean to say, that Mr. Stone intentionally gave the populace a hint to go and break up the meeting? It cannot be otherwise. What, then, will the public think, when informed, that Mr. Stone *did not write the article which Mr. Jay pretends to quote from him*, and that *it was never published editorially in the Commercial Advertiser at all!*

"What will the public, moreover, say of the conduct of Mr. Jay in this matter, when informed of the fact, that in that very same paper of October 2d, 1833, the leading editorial article, written by Mr. Stone himself, *was of directly the opposite tendency, vindicating the right of the abolitionists to hold their meeting, and exhorting every person entertaining opposite or different sentiments, to keep away!* Nay, more: so far from fanning the embers of popular excitement, or writing the paragraph imputed to him, Mr. Stone *protested strongly against an article having obviously such a tendency, which appeared in a morning paper of that day!* Yet such are the facts, and the Commercial Advertiser of October 2d, 1833, shall speak for itself:—The truth of the matter is—and Mr. Jay must have known as much, unless he has been imposed upon, by

> ————————Men that make
> Envy, and crooked malice, nourishment.

And who 'dare bite the best,'—that the passage quoted by Mr. Jay is an *excerpt* from a communication, published as such, and prefaced by the following editorial disclaimer, and expression of our own views:

"*From the Commercial Advertiser of October* 2, 1833.

"Anti-Slavery—the Meeting to-night.—By a notice which has been published in this, as well as other papers, the friends of the immediate abolition of slavery in the United States, are requested to meet, this evening, at Clinton Hall, to form a 'New-York City Anti-Slavery Society.'

"In one sense, the terms of the notice may be construed into a universal invitation of our citizens to attend the meeting, inasmuch as upon the abstract and naked question of an immediate abolition of slavery in the United States, there can be but one voice in the community. We are all, to a man, in favour of the measure, provided it can be immediately accomplished without danger to the whites, without injury to the slaves themselves, without jeoparding the peace and safety of the union, and upon the principles of equal and exact justice to all men. But viewed in all its bearings, there is a wide difference of opinion between those who, *par excellence*, profess themselves *immediate abolitionists*, and the far greater number of our own citizens, equally opposed to slavery, but who desire to pursue some rational plan for its ultimate and certain extinguishment, by which the rights and feelings of the slaveholders shall be consulted, and the condition of the slave improved on his emancipation. And as the gentlemen who have called the meeting are bitterly opposed to the great majority last described, it is fair to suppose their notice to be exclusive in its intention. At any rate, *we have so been inclined to receive it.* Much, therefore, as we lament the calling of such a meeting, at this time, and under existing circumstances, yet *the right of calling it cannot be questioned.* The friends of immediate emancipation, regardless of circumstances and consequences the most fearful and appalling, *have as good a right to their opinions, and to meet, and discuss, and propagate them*, as we have to entertain and inculcate ours. Hence WE HAVE SEEN, WITH REGRET, an inflammatory article in a morning paper, *the evident design and tendency of which is to produce the attendance of persons not intended to be invited, for purposes of opposition, which must result in uproar and confusion.* THIS IS WRONG. The gentlemen calling the meeting are very respectable. They are deeply and sadly in error, according to our views of the great question which is now beginning to agitate the union, with more dangerous throes than at any former period. Still, *they have their rights, and should be allowed to pursue their own measures*, so long as those measures are legal and peaceable, *without molestation from any source. We, therefore, hope* that no persons will attend the meeting, who are opposed to the objects of it, excepting merely as spectators—taking no part, and presenting no obstructions, unless the gentlemen conducting the meeting should feel disposed to present an opportunity for free and manly debate. With this brief expression of *our views*, we give place, at the special request of the writer, to the following communication.

" With what spirit the author was actuated, who, with this article before his eyes, dares to accuse us of giving a ' HINT,' for the purpose of producing a mob, we leave to honest men of any party to decide. We do not believe that Mr. Jay has done this passage of his book entirely himself; but we do not envy the author of the misrepresentation, whoever he may be, the reflections it will one day afford, living or dying. The insinuation, therefore, amounting, in fact, to a direct and positive charge, that the 'hint' was ever given for the assembling of a mob, by the editors of the Commercial Advertiser, though frequently repeated in the volume before us, is UNTRUE ; and we appeal with confidence—not to the garbled quotations or bald assertions of the abolitionists—but to the columns of the paper itself, from the date of the foregoing article until the dis graceful riots which took place *nine months afterwards*, foi proof of our position.

"We may have occasion to recur to this subject again ; but for the present let the foregoing suffice. Meantime, if the author 'knows the things which belongs to his peace,' he will not only lament the publication of such a book, but repent of the evil he has attempted to inflict upon us."

Having thus allowed the Commercial Advertiser, and its editor, to speak for themselves, I shall make no allusion to the extracts you make from the *Courier and Enquirer ;* for its editor, Mr. James Watson Webb, has never, to my knowledge, been identified with the Colonization Society. And from the specimen just furnished of your quotations from the Commercial Advertiser, I confess I have little confidence in the accuracy of your quotations, presuming, as I am bound to do, that in both cases, the extracts are among the materials *furnished you*, for writing your "inquiry," for I will not suspect you of the perversions, and suppression of the truth, of which Colonel Stone has convicted your book. For if I believed you capable of the moral obliquity, which such suspicion would imply, not even your name, or reputation, or profession of Christianity itself, should have induced me to this correspondence.

It is idle, however, to pretend, that the mobs and riots, of which you complain, were occasioned by newspapers, or editors, whether justly, or unjustly, styled colonizationists. Every candid and disinterested witness of those disgraceful scenes, must have attributed them to other, and far more potent causes. It was *actions*, which speak louder than *words*, from which the mischiefs you deplore clearly originated ; and it is unphilosophical and absurd, "to attribute an *effect* to more *causes* than are necessary for its existence." And it requires not the spirit of prophesy to discern, that if there were no Colonization Society in existence, and if all the colonization presses should be silent, the same *conduct* then pursued by your associates of the Anti-Slavery Society, would produce similar results, in any large American community. But as I have elsewhere, in my "acrimonious pamphlet," expressed my opinions on this subject deliberately formed, and published under a deep sense of duty and responsibility, I forbear to enlarge, since my present convictions on that subject remain unchanged.

I must, however, refer for a moment to the extraordinary paragraph on your 112th page, in which, you accuse the society of pouring "obloquy and violence" upon the abolitionists, for the purpose of "INTIMIDATION." The reason of the alleged resort to intimidation is thus expressed:

"Utterly vain is the hope of maintaining the cause of colonization, or of suppressing that of abolition, by *discussion*." And then you add, with a self-complacency, at which even your own party must smile, "*In every instance!* in which colonizationists have ventured to meet their opponents in public disputation, they have invariably retired with *diminished strength*."

If you did not expect, sir, that in your very name, resides "a tower of strength," you might have condescended to have given us some *other* authority for this sweeping clause of your book, by naming some *one* from among "every instance," when public disputation has thus terminated. You do not, surely, pretend to speak from personal knowledge, of "*every instance* in which colonizationists have ventured to meet their opponents in public disputation," and therefore must have given this decision upon the authority of the *Liberator, Emancipator*, or *Evangelist. Par nobile fratrum*, sir, I admit, but neither of these are distinguished for accuracy, else by repeating their dogmas, you had escaped the multiplied mistakes, to which it has been my painful duty to direct your attention. In New-York, where the fact of Mr. Finlay's annihilation of that misguided, but excellent man, Mr. Jocelyn, is so recent, and so well remembered, this assertion of yours provokes a smile. And your "want of information" on this point, has certainly obliterated from your memory, the "public discussion" of the

anniversary week in May last, in Chatham Chapel, in the con-
secutive meetings of the two societies, the result of which has
been, ever since, visible in the *subdued tone*, and "diminished
strength," of the defeated abolitionists.

In conclusion, let me briefly notice your attempt to gainsay
the character of the society as a "*religious* institution," when
you ask, " In what sense can the society be termed a *religious*
one ?" I answer, because it originated in "humanity and benevolence to the oppressed ;"—was founded after solemn and
united *prayer*, for the divine guidance, by Finlay and his associates, whose *religion* prompted them to this good work. That
it is truly a religious society, may be safely inferred from your
own showing, when you say, on p. 116, " The Colonization Society, *unquestionably*, comprises a *vast number* of *as pure and
devoted Christians*, as can be found in this, or any other coun
try !" and again, " that *multitudes* of *religious* men belong to
the Colonization Society *is not denied !*" When, then, you
demand, " in what sense can the society be termed a religious
one," I refer you to these admissions, by which, as you law-
yers are wont to say, you " admit yourself out of court."

But you next affirm, that it is not professedly founded on any
one principle of the gospel of Christ. To this, it might be sufficient to reply, that so long as the "golden rule" is one principle of the gospel of Christ, Christian colonizationists repel
this statement, by declaring, that in colonizing the free people
of colour on the coast of Africa with their own consent, they
are "doing unto others, as they would have others do unto
them," in like circumstances. And in view of that judgment
to which we are hastening, and of which, sir, you take frequent occasion to remind us, I am free to declare, that such is
the "principle of the gospel of Christ," on which my vindication of the society is "founded," and by which I am influenced in common with thousands of my Christian brethren in
the north and the south, of my own and sister denominations.

You tell us, indeed, that the society " extends no one act of
benevolence towards the free blacks in this country," and here
you differ, *toto cœlo*, from your fellow labourer, Charles Stewart, who says,

" For the few coloured people who *prefer* leaving their native country, and emigrating to Africa, it is *unquestionably a great blessing !*" But again, you charge that " the society takes no measures to Christianize Africa, but landing on its shores an ignorant and *vicious* population !" And this, sir, is one of the most unaccountable assertions in your unaccountable book. After the published testimony of British and American visitors to Liberia, touching the general character of the colonists, and with the knowledge you must have of the pious Christians, and devoted ministers of the gospel, whom the society have sent out among the emigrants, I marvel that you should hazard your reputation on such a declaration, that it " takes *no measures* to Christianize Africa, but landing a *vicious* population on its shores." I might point you to the " measures" it has taken to promote schools, and the building of churches, in the colony, as well as the facilities the society offers to Christian missionaries of all denominations, and for which it has received the grateful expression of thanks from more than one board of foreign missions. And I will only add, that the expedition of select emigrants, which lately sailed from New-Orleans, is, of itself, an ample refutation of the accusation of only " landing an ignorant and *vicious* population on the shores of Africa." Allow me again to introduce the contradiction given to you here by that same Charles Stewart, to whom allusion has been made, and who is, even now, itinerating through the *north* and *east*, as a British agent of the *American* Anti-Slavery Society, who says,

" The *highest praise* of the Colonization Society, and a praise which the writer *cordially yields* to it, is *the fact*, that it forms a new centre, whence, as from our Sierra Leone, and the Cape of Good Hope, *civilization and Christianity are radiating* through the adjoining darkness. In this respect, *no praise can equal the worth of these settlements !*"

But lastly, you add, that " it employs no missionary, it sends no Bible, and it cannot point to a single native converted to the faith of Jesus through its instrumentality." That the society is exclusively devoted to the single object of colonization, is, of itself, an ample reason, why it should not depart from its appropriate sphere, yet, "*through its instrumentality*," a great many missionaries have been sent by the societies, devoted to that department, as the names of Cox, Laird, Cloud, Wright, Spaulding, Seys, and Pinney, among the whites, beside a number of coloured missionaries, and male and female teachers of both classes, abundantly prove. Bibles, too, have been sent by the American Bible Society, and the Methodist Episcopal Bible Society, for the use of the colonists; and the British and Foreign Bible Society have availed themselves of the instrumentality of the society for the benefit of the natives, as the following extract of a letter from Governor Pinney will show,

"Several hundred Bibles and Testaments in the Arabic language, have arrived here from England, very lately, a present from the British and Foreign Bible Society. They will give light to many a benighted soul. Some half a dozen were sent to king B. and other chiefs, with the commissioners."

Thus has your "want of information" placed you, sir, again in an unenviable position, since, in the face of such authentic facts, you talk of "no missionary" and "no Bible," in order to prove the society to be "*decidedly* ANTI-CHRISTIAN !" Whether any single native has been "converted through the instrumentality of the society," which you deny, may be judged by the letters of the Rev. Mr. Seys, already before the public, and by the following extract from Mr. James Eden's letter to the ladies of Philadelphia.

"I am happy to inform you, that the Methodist people among the EBOES, [*natives,*] have erected a log meeting house, and now occupy it for public worship. During the evenings of the week, as you pass among their humble dwellings, you may hear the voice of *prayer and praise to God*, in sweet and frequent concert, from many a lowly hut."

Whether any of these are truly converted, can only be decided at the judgment of the great day, but if there are, or ever should be, any natives converted, it is, or will be, effected, through the instrumentality of the society, though itself "employs no missionary, and sends no Bible."

And now, sir, let me ask how you can screen yourself from "the imputation of bigotry or prejudice," if, with these facts before you, you did not scruple to say that "the general influence of the society is decidedly *anti-Christian !*" And how do you reconcile it either with your character or conscience to say,

that this ANTI-CHRISTIAN society contains "*multitudes* of religious men," and "*unquestionably, comprises a* VAST NUMBER
of as pure, and devoted CHRISTIANS, as can be found in this, or
any other country ?"

In reply to your concluding address to the "*Christian* members" of this *anti-Christian* society, I would affectionately say,
that long before your book admonished us, such have been led
"to pause, to examine, and to pray," and the result has been,
that they are colonizationists still. In the language of Gerrit
Smith, Esq., thousands of kindred spirits exclaim—

" If nothing short of the unconditional destruction of the Colonization Society can appease your implacable malevolence
towards it, know, then, that its *friends* are as determined as its
foes. Our determination is fixed—fixed as the love of God,
and the love of man in our hearts—that the Colonization Society, under the blessing of Him who never, even "for a small
moment, has forsaken it," shall continue to live—and to live
too, until the wrongs of the children of Africa amongst us are
redressed, until the slave-trade has ceased, and the dark coasts
which it has polluted and desolated for centuries, are over-
spread with the beautiful and holy fruits of civilization, and
the Christian religion. And, as we fear the judgments of heaven on those who commit great sin, so we dare not desert the
society, and leave Satan to rejoice over the ruin of all this
" work of faith and labour of love."

Finally, let me repeat the reasonable and salutary advice of
Gamaliel, to all who unite with you in your "war of extermination" against the Colonization Society.

"And now I say unto you, Refrain from these men, and let
them alone, for if this counsel, or this work, be of men, it will
come to nought, but if it be of God, ye cannot overthrow it,
lest haply ye be found even to fight against God."

With due respect,
Yours, &c.

PART II.

***

LETTER XI.

Sir,

I come now to your second part, in which you treat of the American Anti-Slavery Society. I have elsewhere attempted to show that this society is "Anti-American in its very nature," by the unanswered argument, that "the *liberty* of the free is not more amply guarded, and fully secured, than is the *slavery* of the enslaved, by the laws of the land," and that an anti-liberty society might, with equal propriety, arrogate the name of *American*. You will understand me to regard the society only in the light of its own constitution, which you quote, in which we are told, in the second article, that its "*object* is the entire abolition of slavery, in the United States," or, as it is expressed, in the same article, "*immediate* abolition, without expatriation." And as you have attempted to identify this society, with the *gradual* abolition societies, with which your illustrious father was associated, I invite your attention to the evidence furnished in his biography, *written by yourself,* that you have unconsciously, and inadvertently, done injustice to the memory of your revered parent. Let me assure you, sir, that no unkind feelings to yourself, mingle in this effort to contrast the opinions of John Jay, the father, with those of William Jay, the son, since both were, doubtless, equally conscientious in their views of duty ; but my only aim is, that the American people may be disabused of the use made of his distinguished name, and choose between the contrary sentiments of the father and the son.

And here let me refer you to a remarkable mistake, in your late publication, on the 146th page, when you ask,

"Did John Jay forfeit the confidence of his countrymen when, during the revolutionary war, he asserted, 'till America comes into this measure, (abolition of slavery,) her prayers to heaven, for liberty, will be impious?'"

For the correction of this mistake, let me now refer you to another work, entitled, "Life of John Jay, by his son *William Jay*." vol. i. page 229, in which the sentence quoted, reads thus:

"An excellent law might be made for New-York, out of the Pennsylvania one, for the GRADUAL abolition of slavery. Till America comes into *this* measure, (gradual abolition,) her prayers to heaven, for liberty, will be impious. This is a strong expression, but it is just. Were I in your legislature, I would prepare a bill for the purpose (of gradual abolition) *with great care*, and I would never cease moving it, till it became a law, or I ceased to be a member."

Here is the unsophisticated sentiment of John Jay, as recorded with your own hand, in 1833. But how strange, that in 1835, with that same hand, you should inadvertently pervert it to express, not merely a different, but an opposite opinion, for you introduce it in a vindication of *immediate* abolition, with which it is totally irrelevant.

This sentiment of your excellent father, which he calls, a "strong expression," is that of nearly *every* colonizationist in the land, and the society is engaged in the very spirit he professed, labouring "for the purpose *with great care*," a feature which *the son* ridicules and condemns, as being the dictate of "expediency."

But as you lay great stress upon the fact, that your venerable father presided over the first society ever formed for the "abolition of slavery," in 1785, though you admit, that it "advocated *gradual* abolition," allow me to refer you to the same life of Jay, vol. i. page 231, for the title of that society which was, "The society for promoting the manumission of slaves, and protecting such of them as have been, or may be, liberated."

Now it is plain that there is no one point of parallel between this society, and that to which you attempt a forced analogy, and though it undoubtedly exercised a moral influence in promoting voluntary, and *gradual* abolition, yet, in this respect, it precisely *resembles the Colonization Society :* and for the same proscribed reason of " expediency," the name and object of the society does not recognize abolition, as the *direct* action which it should exert, but, like our institution, it relied upon the moral influence which should be consequent on its success.

I must suppose, sir, that when you published the life of your father, in 1833, you had not yet been innoculated with " immediate abolitionism," much less did you intend to become the vindicator of the American Anti-Slavery Society, or contemplate the denunciation of the American Colonization Society, within two years afterwards.   And, if I err in this supposition, you will, at least, admit that it is a very natural one on my part, since the former work furnishes facts, and arguments, in relation to John Jay, which place his son, William Jay, upon the *antipodes* of the present controversy ; for I hesitate not to say, that the extracts I shall make from your own biography of your father, will prove an able and triumphant vindication of the Colonization Society, its principles, and practice.   At the same time, these extracts will show the estimate which John Jay would have formed of the Anti-Slavery Society, had he lived, to witness its origin.   That he would have deplored the present vindication of the latter, and aspersion of the former, and especially by his son and biographer, cannot admit of a doubt.

To a few of these extracts, let me now invite your attention. And first, did John Jay believe with the Anti-Slavery Society, that " slaveholding was a HEINOUS CRIME in the sight of God ?" Let us turn to his biography, and we shall answer this question, on your own authority ?   In vol. i. p. 230, we learn, that in the year 1779, he purchased a negro boy at Martinico, named Benoit, and that nine years afterward, he executed a formal manumission of this negro boy, on condition of a continuance to serve his master "with a common and reasonable degree of fidelity, for three years from the date hereof, he shall ever afterward be a free man."   And, as the date of this document is March 21st, 1784, it is manifest, that this boy continued in slavery until two years after Mr. Jay became the president of the Manumission Society.

But let me now direct your attention to page 235, of this same volume of the biography of John Jay, in which we find the following fact, by which it appears, that he continued to *purchase and hold slaves*, 13 years afterwards.

"In the year 1798, John Jay being called on by the United States Marshal for an account of his taxable *property*, he accompanied *a list of his slaves* with the following observations :

" I purchase slaves, and manumit them at proper ages, and when their faithful services shall have afforded a reasonable retribution."*

How many slaves he held, and whether he continued to be a slaveholder until the abolition of the system from the state, does not appear. But surely, he did not then believe " slaveholding to be a *heinous crime* in the sight of God ;" much less would he have relished the denunciation of anti-slavery orators and preachers, as being guilty of "*robbery, piracy,* and *murder !*"

On the same page, we find three sentences worthy of preservation. The first is from yourself, in which you say of the Manumission Society, over which your father presided,

" The society neither *expected, nor attempted* to effect, any *sudden* alteration in the *laws relating to slavery,* but its exertions were directed to the protection of manumitted slaves, and to the education of coloured children."

Now, contrast this with your reprobation of those very "laws," and your argument for their immediate " instant abolition," and you will be ashamed of your attempted analogy between those societies and that whose cause you espouse.

The second extract from this page, is from John Jay, who speaks of the utility of that society in promoting gradual abolition, and gives his " picture of American slavery," which is vastly unlike yours :

" Manumissions daily become more common among us, and the *treatment* which *slaves in general* meet with, in this state, is very little different from that of other servants."

But a third extract, is from your own testimony, in reference

---

* This is what the first annual report of the American Anti-Slavery Society calls a " wretched mockery of justice."

to the "*necessity*" imposed upon your father, to "purchase slaves;"—though on pp. 97 and 98 of your present work, you call this " necessity" the "*tyrant's plea*," for "trampling upon human rights, and outraging the plainest principles of *justice and humanity*." But let us attend to the extract.

" As free servants became more common, he, (John Jay,) was *gradually* relieved from the NECESSITY of purchasing slaves; and the two last which he manumitted, he retained for many years in his family, at the customary wages." From this, we learn, that if free servants had not become more common, this *necessity to purchase slaves* would have continued, nor would he have been even "gradually relieved" from it. If this be not an "apology for slavery" in the south, where free servants are not common, none has ever been given by colonizationists, and I marvel that you should have so soon forgotten it, in condemning this "tyrant's plea."

The following merited tribute to your honoured father, on page 232, vol. i. of his life, is a striking exhibition of the wisdom of the efforts for *gradual* abolition, which you so violently denounce ;

" It was *only* by *slow degrees*, and through the *patient* and *persevering* efforts of Mr. Jay, and a few other zealous pioneers, that the obstacles which retarded the progress of freedom, were *gradually removed*, and slavery exterminated from the soil of New-York."

What a reproof to the theory of immediate abolitionism have you here furnished, and how conclusively have you refuted in 1833, the book you have written in 1835.

Some idea of the *slow and gradual* progress of abolition, in our own state, may be gathered by the following extracts from vol. i. pp. 389 and 396. I invite your attention to the words italicised, as evincing that John Jay wisely adopted the policy of expediency, which you reprobate in your present book, as involving a " lamentable compromise of principle."

" When we recollect the sentiments uniformly avowed by Governor Jay in relation to slavery, it may seem singular that no proposition for its abolition was contained in his speech. It was no doubt *omitted from the conviction that*, in the present state of politics, such a proposition emanating from him, would enlist the spirit of party in opposition to a measure, against which the *préjudices* of a large portion of the community were already arrayed. He, therefore, deemed it *most prudent* that the measure should originate with the legislature. Accordingly, a few days after the commencement of the session, a member of the lower house, and an intimate friend of the governor's, asked leave to introduce a bill for the *gradual abolition* of slavery. This request, which is usually granted as a matter of course, was unexpectedly resisted, and leave was finally given by a small majority. The vote evinced the strong repugnance felt by the house, even to take the subject into consideration. The bill underwent a protracted discussion, and was ultimately defeated by a resolve, that it would be unjust to deprive any citizen of his PROPERTY, without a reasonable pecuniary compensation, at the expense of the state. It was well understood by all, that on this condition, it was impracticable to abolish slavery ; and no further attempt to carry the bill was made during the session. An important point had, however, been gained by its introduction. The discussion had awakened public attention to the subject, and the friends of justice and humanity were well assured, that the more the evils of slavery were exposed, the sooner would the public demand its extinction." Vol. i. p. 389.

"In January, 1797, the legislature again assembled, and a bill was brought into the senate for the *gradual* abolition of slavery. The opposition to this bill was less open than that which it had experienced in the other house the preceding winter, but it was not, perhaps, less insidious. Its consideration was postponed from time to time, by a hostile majority, till the session expired without a vote being taken on its merits." Vol. i. p. 396.

To show that John Jay had not changed his opinions, as late as 1819, I refer you to page 452 of his Life, vol. i., where he says, in a letter to Elias Boudinot, "I concur in the opinion that slavery ought to be *gradually diminished,* and *finally* abolished, in all the states." And this was two years after he and others, had been successful in effecting gradual abolition in the state of New-York.

But I would now invite your attention to the negociations of

John Jay, and the provisions of the treaty he made with Great Britain, for proof that he regarded slaves as *property*, which you regard a high crime and misdemeanour in the Colonization Society and its friends. The following sentence will be sufficient for my purpose, though many more might be furnished to the same purpose.

"The treaty stipulated that his Britannic Majesty should withdraw his armies, &c. without carrying away any *negroes or other* PROPERTY of the American inhabitants." Vol. i. p. 327. And by a paragraph in vol. ii. p. 221, we learn that the negociation terminated in the recovery of the value of "those negroes who were *bona fide* the *property* of Americans when the war ceased."

In vol. ii. p. 317, we have a correspondence between Wilberforce and Jay, on the subject of the slave-trade, in which reference is had to the "African Institution," with the Duke of Gloucester at its head, many members of both houses of parliament, &c. for the single object of "promoting civilization and improvement in Africa;" and it will be seen, that Mr. Jay applauds the society for the precise reason, that multitudes in this country rejoice in the Colonization Society. He says,

"*The* patrons of the African Institution, certainly *do honour* and will probably do more than ordinary *good* to Britain, against whom complaints have ascended both from Asia and Africa. It is pleasing to see a nation *kindly extending the blessings of Christianity and civilization* to Africa."

But the following letter, as you inform us, from the pen of John Jay, to the British Abolition Society, is also found on page 232, vol. i., and will be found to express the precise sentiments of colonizationists against which you declaim as giving evidence that they are governed by "*expediency* instead of principle," that they "excuse and justify slavery," and it contains in the strongest language, the conviction of its author, that *immediate abolition* could not rationally be expected. He writes like a statesman who knew and loved his country, and felt the delicacies and difficulties of the subject, in view of "local interests and local prejudices," which he acknowledged to be entitled to respect, because of "the importance of union" for any

measure of success. It will be seen with what gentleness and
point, he rebukes the British for their interference, by remind-
ing them kindly of their own national participation in the oppression, while he deplores that of his own country, and attributes it to the "particular circumstances in several of the
states." He alludes to the fact, that slavery has become "incorporated in the *civil institutions* and domestic economy of a
whole people, and though an *error*, difficult to eradicate." How
different from the sentiments, language, and spirit of his son,
the reader will judge.

"GENTLEMEN,

"Our society has been favoured with your letter of the 1st of
May last, and are happy that efforts so honourable to the nation are making in your country to promote the cause of justice
and humanity relative to the Africans. That they who know
the value of liberty, and are blessed with the enjoyment of it,
ought not to subject others to slavery, is, like most *other moral
precepts*, more generally admitted in *theory* than observed in
practice. This will continue to be too much the case while
men are impelled to action by their passions rather than their
reason, and while they are more solicitous to acquire wealth
than to do as they would be done by. Hence it is that India
and Africa experience unmerited *oppression* from *nations* who
have been long distinguished by their attachment to their civil
and religious liberties; but who have expended not much less
blood and treasure in *violating the rights of others*, than in de-
fending their own. The United States are far from being irre-
proachable in this respect. It undoubtedly is very inconsistent
with their declarations on the subject of human rights to permit a single slave to be found within their jurisdiction, and we
confess the justice of your strictures on that head.

"Permit us, however, to observe, that although consequences
ought not to deter us from doing what is right, yet that it is *not
easy to persuade men in general* to act on that magnanimous
and disinterested principle. It is well known that *errors*, either
in opinion or practice, *long entertained or indulged, are difficult to eradicate,* and particularly so when they have become,
as it were, incorporated in the *civil institutions and domestic
economy of a whole people.*

"Prior to the late revolution, the great majority, or rather the great body of our people, had been so long accustomed to the *practice and convenience of having slaves*, that very few among them ever *doubted the propriety and rectitude of it.* Some liberal and conscientious men had, indeed, by their conduct and writings, drawn the lawfulness of slavery into *question*, and they made converts to that opinion; but the number of those converts compared with the people at large, was then *very inconsiderable.* Their doctrines prevailed by *almost insensible degrees*, and was like the little lump of leaven which was put into three measures of meal: *even at this day*, the whole mass is far from being leavened, though we have good reason to hope and to believe that if the natural operations of truth are constantly *watched and assisted*, but NOT *forced and precipitated*, the end we ALL aim at will *finally* be attained in this country.

" The convention who formed and recommended the new constitution had an arduous task to perform, especially as *local interests*, and in some measure *local prejudices*, were to be *accommodated.* Several of the states conceived that *restraints* on slavery might be *too rapid* to consist with their *particular circumstances;* and the *importance of union* rendered it *necessary* that their wishes on that head should, in some degree, be gratified.

" It gives us pleasure to inform you, that a disposition favourable to our views and wishes prevails more and more, and that it has already had an *influence on our laws.* When it is considered how many of the legislators in the different states are *proprietors of slaves*, and what opinions and *prejudices* they have imbibed on the subject from their infancy, a SUDDEN AND TOTAL STOP TO THIS SPECIES OF OPPRESSION IS NOT TO BE EXPECTED.

" We will cheerfully co-operate with you in endeavouring to *procure* advocates for the same cause in *other countries*, and perfectly approve and commend your establishing a correspondence in France. It appears to have produced the desired effect; for Mons. De Warville, the secretary of a society for the like benevolent purpose at Paris, is now here; and comes instructed to establish a correspondence with us, and to collect such information as may promote our common views. He delivered to our society an extract from the minutes of your proceedings, dated 8th of April last, recommending him to our attention; and upon that occasion they passed the resolutions of which the enclosed are copies.

"We are much obliged by the pamphlets enclosed with your letter, and shall constantly make such communications to you as may appear to us interesting.

"By a report of the committee for superintending the school we have established in this city for the education of negro children, we find that proper attention is paid to it, and that scholars are now taught in it. By the laws of this state, masters may now liberate healthy slaves of a proper age without giving security that they shall not become a parish charge; and the exportation, as well as importation of them, is prohibited. The state has also manumitted such as became its property by confiscation; and we have reason to expect that the maxim, that every man, of whatever colour, is to be *presumed to be free until the contrary be shown*, will prevail in our courts of justice. *Manumissions daily become more common among us;* and the *treatment* which *slaves in general* meet with in this state is *very little different from that of other socities.*

"I have the honour to be, gentlemen,

"Your humble servant,

"John Jay,

"President of the Society for promoting the Manumission of Slaves."

You here add,

"The society neither expected nor attempted to effect any *sudden* alteration in the *laws relating to slavery*, but its exertions were chiefly directed to the *protection of manumitted slaves*, and to the education of coloured children. Mr. Jay continued at the head of the society until he became chief justice of the United States, when, thinking it possible that questions might be brought before him in which the society was interested, he deemed it proper to dissolve his official connexion with it."

With this exhibition of the contrariety of views between father and son, and between your own views in 1833 and in 1835, I submit to the reader the decision, which is entitled to the greater confidence,—the late John Jay, chief justice in the Supreme Court of the United States, or—William Jay, associate judge of Westchester County Court!

And as you have yourself furnished the public with the mirror which reflects this exhibition of yourself, you cannot justly complain that I have " held it up to nature."

With due respect,

Yours, &c.

LETTER XII.

Sir,

In the abstract you have given of the "laws relating to slavery," in the several states, you have not only falsely attributed those laws to the Colonization Society, or its influence, but after a "picture of American slavery" as seen in these laws, you say :—

"This is the system which the Colonization Society *excuses*, and which it CONTENDS *ought to be perpetual*, rather than its victims should enjoy their rights in 'the white man's land.'"

And here is another specimen of the reckless dogmatism with which you assail the victim of your wrath. I have already shown, that the Colonization Society does not excuse the system, in any sense in which John Jay does not excuse it, and you will not now persist in the latter allegation, for I am persuaded that you had forgotten your own testimony on that subject. But when or where does the Colonization Society *contend* that the system ought to be perpetual, or when did that society call this "the white man's land." You must know upon reflection, that these charges have no foundation but in your own imagination. and even the authority of your name will fail in gaining them confidence in any community.

The description you give of the "principles and designs of the abolitionists," would perhaps gain credence, but for the single fact, that they have avowed "principles and designs" essentially different in their own publications, and the public therefore cannot receive your testimony on that subject, while your "want of information" is so apparent. And here you cannot object to the application of the *lex talionis*, and therefore I invite your attention to the evidence furnished by the official publications of the American Anti-slavery Society, holding that society responsible only for such, though I might justly insist upon all the abominable sentiments which from time to time have

disgraced the columns of the Liberator, Emancipator, Evangelist, *et id omne genus.*

Now you represent these *innocent* abolitionists as *only* affirm-
ing that *slavery is sinful,* to which you know the Colonization
Society virtually subscribe, when they call it a *"moral evil,"*
and John Jay, when he calls it an *"error."* But what says
their constitution.

"Slaveholding (not slavery) is a *heinous crime* in the sight
of God." And instead of "arguments addressed to the understandings and consciences of their fellow citizens, to convince
them of the duty and policy of immediate emancipation," as
you say on p. 136, the constitution proves, that it is to convict
them of this *"heinous crime,"* that these arguments are used.
See article ii.

But again you say, "the MEANS by which the society will endeavour to secure to the blacks, an equality of civil and religious privileges, are frankly avowed to be, *the encouragement
of their intellectual, moral, and religious improvement, and
the removal of existing prejudices against them."* But what
are the *means* which their first annual report proposes for this
object? Let us see.

"Let some of our higher institutions of learning trample on
the *cord of caste!* and open their doors to all, without *distinction of complexion!"*

"Let it be the glory of our *sons and daughters,* to have been
educated in seminaries which were open to worthy applicants,
without regard to complexion!"

But you seem to have forgotten the *means** which are em-

---

* Among the MEANS used by the Anti-Slavery Society, and its
friends, for the promotion of their objects, is their proposed *exclusion
of Christian Ministers from their pulpits,* and the like *exclusion of
Christian professors from the ordinances of the Lord's house,* by making
slaveholding a test of communion, in the northern churches. This
unscriptural measure is not only advocated in the anti-slavery press,
but has been actually introduced into several of the professed churches
of Christ in the City of New-York, and elsewhere, and is strenuously recommended to the adoption of all the churches in the non-
slaveholding states.

By such *means,* it is expected to alienate ministers from the people
of their charge, distract and divide churches, alienate the affection
and confidence of northern from southern Christians, and thus, to

ployed throughout your book, and in which all the funds of your society, and all the eloquence of your agents, have been expended. The whole army of immediate abolitionists have adopted, as their motto, the title of Mr. Cropper's book, " *The extinction of the American Colonization Society, the first step toward the abolition of slavery.*" This is the MEANS on which you all build your hopes, and to which you concentrate your efforts, and yet you have entirely overlooked the " overthrow of the colonization delusion," in your exposition of the means used for the attainment of the objects of abolitionists. On page 90 of your own book, you inadvertently avow this as the principal means, for you call upon abolitionists to meet the Colonization Society with " *unrelenting hostility,* and to labour *without rest,* and *without weariness,* for its *entire prostration ;*" and yet, on page 136, you have forgotten all this, and in a " *frank* avowal" of the means used by the society, and of their principles and designs, you carefully omit to mention it Is this " principle, or expediency ?"

But suffer me now, to examine a few of the " ARGUMENTS addressed to the *understandings and consciences of slaveholders,*" by the Anti-Slavery Society.

" The truth is, and it must be suppressed no longer, we have been hired to abet oppression, to be the tools of tyrants—to look on coolly, while 2,000,000 of our brethren have been stripped of every right, and *worse than murdered !*"—1st *Annual Report.*

" The man who seizes another in New-York, and drags him into bondage, (alluding to the legal arrest of a fugitive slave, under the constitution of the United States,) *whatever laws he*

---

use the language of George Thompson, the British agent of the American Anti-Slavery Society, who is now propagating his creed of political and religious nullification through the northern and eastern states, " to split the great Methodist prop," and "the great Presbyterian prop," to which, he says, " granite is nothing !" and the " great Baptist prop," &c. which, he says, unitedly support slavery in the United States. This is one of the *means* which Mr. Jay must include in those " frankly avowed," and he will scarcely persuade the reader to believe, that Mr. Frelinghuysen was in error, when he said, they " seek to destroy our happy union," by all his declamation, or sophistry either.

may have in his favour, is to be regarded as a ROBBER AND PI-RATE !"—1st *Annual Report*.

"Slaveholding is *piracy*, equally atrocious with slave-trading; and if there is any difference in criminality, slaveholding is the WORST OF THE TWO !"—*Speech of Mr. Phelps*.

"The slave states are *Sodoms*, and almost every village family a *brothel !*"—*Speech of Mr. Thome*.

"Jesus Christ was a *coloured man !*"—*Sermon of the Rev. Dr. Cox*.

"Suppose the *constitution* did sanction slavery? What then ? While there is a God in heaven, *can we be bound* by any *compacts* of our own, or any ENACTMENTS of our fellow worms, to sin against Him ?"—*Speech of Rev. Mr. May*.

The following *arguments !* are from the "Declaration of the Anti-Slavery Convention."

"The *guilt of this nation* is *unequalled* by any other on the face of the earth."

"*Every American citizen*, who retains a human being in in-voluntary bondage, is (according to scripture) a *man stealer !*"*

"All those LAWS which are now in force, admitting the right of slavery, are, *before God*, NULL AND VOID."

And now look at the "*arguments*" of that "much calum-niated" individual, as you call him, Mr. Garrison, "to the *un-derstanding and conscience !*"

"The Colonization Society is a creature *without brains, eyeless, unnatural, hypocritical, relentless, unjust.*"

"Ye *crafty calculators !* ye *hard hearted, incorrigible sin-ners !* ye *greedy and relentless robbers !* ye *contemners of justice* and *mercy !* ye *trembling, pitiful, pale-faced usurpers !* my *soul* spurns you with unspeakable *disgust !*"

What a specimen of "great *moral principles*, frankly and unequivocally avowed !" and how powerful must be the effect of such "arguments" as these; "upon the understanding and conscience !" And yet, "such are the principles and designs of those who are now designated as abolitionists," who, you say, suffer "unmerited and unmeasured reproach."

After the reader has perused the foregoing extracts, he will

---

* Query ? Was John Jay a "*man stealer*," while president of the Manumission Society ?

be surprised, that you should have written an entire chapter, to prove that the immediate abolitionists are not "fanatics." I should not, sir, require any testimony, other than that contained in your own book, to convict you, and all the anti-slavery party, of *fanaticism*, before any candid and intelligent jury. It is the purest fanaticism that was ever exhibited in the history of our race. It blinds the eyes, perverts the intellect, destroys the memory, blunts the moral sense, hardens the heart, sears the conscience, annihilates the religion of its votaries, and practically teaches, that while "slaveholding is a heinous crime," "bearing false witness" is *no crime at all!* If this be not fanaticism, and of all this, your book affords melancholy demonstration, then I know not where it is to be found.

In your attempted vindication of the Anti-Slavery Society from the charge of being "*incendiaries and traitors,*" you quote from Jefferson, Jay, and Franklin, while you must know, that each of the sentiments, imputed to them, were expressed in favour of "*gradual* abolition," and though you lay great stress upon them, they are entirely irrelevant. When, therefore, you attempt to show contrariety between those gentlemen, and Messrs. T. Frelinghuysen, Chancellor Walworth, and David B. Ogden, Esq., you grievously misrepresent them. The proof of the charges, made by the three gentlemen last named, will be found in the preceding extracts from anti-slavery publications. Mr. Frelinghuysen justly accuses the immediate abolitionists of "seeking to destroy our happy union;"—Chancellor Walworth charges upon them, "contemplating a violation of the rights of property, secured by the constitution they have sworn to support; and of pursuing measures which would lead to a civil war;" and David B. Ogden, Esq., declares your doctrine of "immediate emancipation to be direct and palpable *nullification.*" These men are your accusers, and you admit one of them to be "deservedly distinguished for his *piety*, talents, and station;" another, to be one of our "*most estimable* citizens;" and the third, to be "a gentleman whose legal eminence, and *purity of character, justly* give to his opinions peculiar weight;" and yet you hope to gainsay such evidence, by the bare assertion, that they make "charges unsupported by a *particle of testimony!*"

Surely your abolitionism has placed you, sir, in an unenviable predicament, when you are constrained, in self-vindication, to hold up such men as these are, by your own showing, to the indignation of your fellow citizens and fellow Christians.   And ought you not to " pause, to ponder, and to pray," lest, haply, you be yourself withering beneath that very fanaticism which you so earnestly disclaim ? Surely, however you may repel the charge of *political* nullification, you furnish palpable evidence, that your creed nullifies the courtesies of good fellowship and Christian comity ; and I cannot but regret, that " a man, possessing the power to do so much good, should, from 'want of information,' so grievously misapply it."

With due respect,
Yours, &c.

LETTER XIII.

Sir,

Your chapter on the subject of "Slavery under the Authority of Congress," next claims my attention. And as slavery in the District of Columbia is a subject almost annually calling forth rebuke and remonstrance from various parts of the union, and as so large a portion of the public press has been for many years occupied with appeals to congress for its abolition in the district, you might have spared yourself the details you furnish touching this department of the subject, if you had not designed to add another to your series of unfounded aspersions of the Colonization Society, this unfortunate victim of your relentless hostility.

Year after year have the leading members and friends of the Colonization Society memorialized congress to abolish slavery and the domestic slave-trade at the seat of the Federal Government, and those who have watched the gradual improvement in the temper with which such memorials have been viewed at Washington, cannot have failed to perceive that until two or three years past, the aspect of this interesting and important subject has been brightening, and, as is believed by many friends in both houses, had the subject continued to be brought before our national legislature, unconnected with any violent or offensive attitude on the part of the memorialists, by this time, the result so desirable for the character of the nation, and so dear to the friends of humanity, might probably have been attained. But, alas! in our evil day, the American Anti-Slavery Society has most indiscreetly taken this subject out of other and better hands, and, after having laboured to agitate the country by violent denunciation, and created among the wisest of our statesmen apprehensions of a dissolution of the union, by arraying, so far as in them lies, the north against the south, and thus rousing prejudices and distrust on the part of those who are so circumstanced, that they are morbidly sensitive when the subject of slavery is touched in congress, this society has taken a prominent part in presenting the late memorial.

Under such circumstances, it was hardly to be expected that the petition would have been disposed of by *quietly* laying it on the table, and the fact that this course was taken, is an evidence of the forbearance of those who felt keenly in reference to the participation, by the Anti-Slavery Society, in getting up the petition. This society having rendered themselves obnoxious to a large portion of the members of the national legislature, by the character of their publications, in becoming petitioners for the abolition of slavery in the district, they give to that important and desirable object the character of a *party measure*, and, by consequence, alienate those who would otherwise favour it. And I have reason to know by personal intercourse and correspondence with members of both houses, that the friends and devoted advocates of the object, despair of success in its attainment, so long as the Anti-Slavery Society are among its prominent supporters. In truth, sir, there can be little doubt that the feeling excited by immediate abolitionists will for many years delay, if it do not utterly prevent, the success of any future memorial. And if you, sir, desire to see the day when slavery shall no longer disgrace the District of Columbia, let the influence you have acquired with the party by becoming their apologist be exerted to induce them to abstain from all interference with the subject, since such interference on their part will be mischievous if not fatal to the object.

But although this measure has long interested the hearts and called forth the efforts of colonizationists in various parts of the country, before the anti-slavery party had awakened from their slumbers, yet you say that you "appeal in vain to the *benevolence* of the Colonization Society?" And this too in the same paragraph in which you say that "no power on earth but congress can remedy the evil!" And yet it seems you blame the Colonization Society for the legislation of congress, as well as that of the states. Let me once more tell you that the Colonization Society, as such, has no authority to interfere in the subject, although its members may and do express their opinions, and exert their influence individually to rouse congress to action on the subject of slavery in the District of Columbia, and the late memorial will demonstrate that a large proportion of the signers were colonizationists, who did not withhold their names from the agents of the Anti-Slavery Society, though they feared the effect of that party upon the object.

You need not then have vindicated your associates from the charge of " wild fanaticism," or pretend that they have been branded as "traitors and nullifiers" for having endeavoured to influence congress on this subject, for your own book furnishes evidence that the Pennsylvania and New-York Legislatures have exercised the same right, and it is one against which there is, there can be, no objection, and hence all you have said on this subject is perfectly idle. Thousands of colonizationists are ready to unite with you in labouring to promote the abolition of slavery in the district, if this were your "single object," and it would be sufficient to call forth all your energies and all your patience too. The cruelties and abominations of the "licensed traffic in human flesh," which you depict in strong language, as existing under the shade of the Capitol, and the reprobation of this disgrace to our common country, I feel to be called for, nor do I believe that the members of the Coloni zation Society generally feel less, or are prepared to do less for its extinction, than yourself or your associates. On this subjec, we only differ as to the means likely to produce the end. would continue to expose its enormities, and appeal to the na tional legislature by annual petitions, nor would I cease to urg the importance of the subject until congress should be gradually prepared for a gradual system of abolition, like that of New York, which was produced in this very way, and has resulte, in the honoor and freedom of the empire state. But I woul. deprecate all rash declamation and intemperate haste, as inex pedient and mischievous, calculated to retard if not totally de feat the object proposed. *Suaviter in modo, fortiter in re,* the motto which ought ever to be present in such an underta king, and *must* be regarded in order to success.

But your next chapter on Slavery under State Authority, con tains a defence of the society against the charge of "wishin congress to abolish slavery in the states." The disclaimer o

his wish was hardly called for, much less the specious argument you have attempted, for I never recollect seeing it insinuated until I found it in your book. And yet you quote from the
Hon. Daniel Webster, a certificate that he " does not know any
persons, and is sure there are very few, who suppose that congress has any power over the states on the subject of slavery."
Surely this is but a testimony to the intelligence of the north,
which was rendered necessary only by the impeachment of
their understanding, which Mr. W. repels. But you must not
expect, sir, that your readers can be induced by a disclaimer of
.nis creature of your own imagination, to acquit the Anti-Slavery Society of nullification, of which Mr. Ogden justly accuses it, and for which you load him with obloquy. You were
ever charged with wishing *congress* to nullify the state laws,
and your quotations from the reports of the Anti-Slavery Society to disprove this are entirely uncalled for. You are charged
with being *yourselves* nullifiers, without the aid of congress,
and I respectfully invite your attention to the proof. The fol-
.owing quotation from the official anti-slavery declaration is
irrefragable evidence.

" All those LAWS which are *now in force*, admitting the right
of slavery, are therefore, before God, utterly NULL and *void !*"

Here, I humbly submit, is a "solemn declaration," with "all
the pomp and circumstance" which a *convention* could give it,
of palpable and overt *nullification !* It is both *political* and
moral nullification. Suppose any body of men were to orga-
nize in a similar manner, and issue a "declaration," that "all
those laws which are now in force, admitting the right [*of
liberty of speech and of the press*] are before God utterly *null
and void,*" would you hesitate to call such a body of men
conspirators against the liberty of this nation, or to denounce the
authors of such an act as *nullifiers ?* And suppose they were
to defend themselves, by saying, that they never " wished
congress to interfere with the states !" would this be regarded
in any other light than adding insult to injury ? The parallel
is clear, the analogy perfect.

But an her instance of nullification contemplated by the society, and to effect which they *do* solicit the interference of

congress, notwithstanding your disclaimer, and authorities, is contained in this "famous declaration," as follows:

"We maintain that CONGRESS *has a right*, and is SOLEMNL BOUND, to suppress the domestic slave-trade *between the several states !*"

Now compare this with the several quotations you give to prove that the Anti-Slavery Society would deprecate the "inter ference of congress on the subject of slavery as a violation o the national compact." Is it no "interference with the slav states *in relation to slavery*," to "suppress the domestic slave trade between the several states," which the society declare congress not only to have a right to do, but to be "solemnly bound' "to exercise it." Friend Hubbard and Mr. Gurley, then, have some reason to say abolitionists are endeavouring to "cause the national legislation to bear directly on the slaveholders,'' and in "a great degree *against and in defiance of the will of the south.*" If you have never before "seen an attempt to prove it," you will please consider this a feeble one, and which. if I thought it needful, I might strengthen by still further quotations. I think, however, you will find it difficult to evade the force of those here presented, and it is clear, that "Chancellor Walworth, and his two associates," have *some foundation* for the opinions against which you so earnestly protest.

After having abjured the sentiments attributed to your society, to which I have just alluded, you "next attempt a justification of the anti-slavery efforts made exclusively *at the North* where there are *no slaves.*" And here you have the following extraordinary sentiment.

"If it could be *foreseen*, that *no slave* in any of the states, would *ever be liberated* through the influence of northern anti-slavery societies, there would still remain great and glorious objects to stimulate their zeal, to employ all their energies, and *abundantly to reward !* all their labours."

So, then, the labours of the American ANTI-SLAVERY Society, and all its auxiliaries, may be "*abundantly* rewarded," in "NO SLAVE should *ever be liberated !*" This provokes a sm.le ; 2,245,144 slaves, "compelled to live without God, and to die w.th out hope," and yet a society, professing to be *anti-slavery*, and naving a " single object," the " entire abolition of slavery," " immediate abolition, without expatriation !" and yet we are told, _n the first year of its existence, that all its labours would be *abundantly* rewarded, though " *no slave* in any of the states .hall ever be liberated !" Surely this " powerful institution," would be " very thankful for small favours !" Truly, I have always been persuaded, that the " frank avowal" of the Constitution of the American Anti-Slavery Society did not express its real object, nor could I convince myself, that if they were *only* anti-slavery they would have laboured so long without having liberated a single slave. But, I confess, sir, that I was scarcely prepared for this " frank avowal," though the fact does not surprise me, yet I fear you have disclosed it rather indiscreetly, and I should not marvel if it were to call forth another " disclaimer."

The reader need not be surprised at this strange inconsistency, for although called " Anti-Slavery," and its object being " *immediate abolition,*" yet it will be *abundantly* rewarded, though *no slave* be liberated, as we learn by this paragraph, if it shall only succeed in the *great and glorious* object, employing *all* its energies, that of counteracting " the baneful influence of the *Colonization Society* at the north !" And the " Black Act of Connecticut," together with "Judge Dagget's decision," are here referred to as being the subjects, the " *immediate abolition*" of which will *abundantly reward* the anti-slavery society, " if *no slave* in any of the states be liberated *through its influence !*" You have elsewhere declared " unrelenting hostility to the Colonization Society," and instructed your associates in the duty of labouring, " without weariness, and without rest, for its *entire prostration.*" But I did not expect that you would have the " moral courage" to avow that this is your *chief,* if not your *only object,* and that the Anti-Slavery Society is *only* an Anti-Colonization Society, and may receive an *abundant reward,* without liberating a single slave.

What then are we to think of the moving appeals you have made to heaven and earth, in behalf of the millions of slaves who are all " living without God, and dying without hope," while you are *abundantly rewarded,* without giving freedom to one of them, if you can only " prostrate" the Colonization Society !

Let me assure you, sir, that the members of the Colonization Society, though they may regard the extinction of the American Anti-Slavery Society, as a "consummation devoutly to be wished," for the sake of the interests of humanity and religion, and the regeneration of Africa ; yet no one among them would be "abundantly rewarded," if *no slave* in any of the states should be liberated through their influence. Nay, verily, such are our convictions of the evil of slavery, and the duty of promoting its abolition, that I but speak the sentiments of tens of thousands, whom you vilify as colonizationists, when I say, that we view the system of *slavery* with "unrelenting hostility," and mean to "labour without weariness, and without rest, for its *gradual* and entire abolition." This is our anti-slavery creed, and we will never be *abundantly rewarded,* while within our country, or on any other spot of earth, there lives a fellow man who calls his brother *slave!* You, then, and those who think with you, are not "*anti-slavery enough*" for me, and from such I turn away, nor would I own as a colonizationist any professed friend of the African race, who would consider himself "abundantly rewarded," or satisfied in any respect, while a single slave remains in involuntary bondage. And although the Colonization Society, as such, cannot interfere, and *ought not,* to exert any *direct* action upon the subject, because contrary to the letter of its constitution, yet the *moral influence* its success exerts in favour of voluntary abolition, is mighty in its operation, and successful in its results.

It is amazing, sir, to your best friends, to discover the unhappy evidences of the infatuation of your mind, when you could write such sentences as the following, and what is superlatively ludicrous, persuade yourself that these are the fruits of northern abolitionism.

"The consciences of southern Christians so long lulled by the *opiate* of *colonization,* are AWAKENING to duty. Southern divines are *beginning to acknowledge* the sinfulness of slavery, and recent slaveholders are *now* proclaiming the safety and duty of immediate emancipation. The *whole nation* has been roused from its lethargy, and in almost every circle and neighbourhood, the subject of abolition is attracting attention ; the violence and persecution experienced by abolitionists instead of suppressing, has promoted discussion, and they have reason to hope, that slavery will *ultimately* be abolished, by the voluntary action of the south, in compliance with the dictates of policy and duty !"

What a mighty moral engine is colonization ! How wonderful that this powerful *opiate* should " *lull* the consciences of *southern Christians* and *northern divines*," and throw this " *whole nation* into the profoundest *lethargy*." But how infinitely *more mighty*, is your anti-slavery *antidote !* Already Christians, divines, and the whole nation, are "awakening" from their " lethargy," and "beginning" to live ! Had you found it convenient to furnish some instances, or even a single example, produced by abolitionism in proof of this ridiculous conceit, in the shape of a liberated slave, colonizationists themselves would rejoice with you. But alas ! in the absence of such proof, you content yourself and immediate abolitionists, with *hoping* that " slavery will be ULTIMATELY abolished by the *voluntary* action of the south," in the precise language and spirit of colonizationists from the beginning, and in the strongest possible terms you abandon *immediateism*, for *gradualism*, and only hope for voluntary abolition, and this *ultimately !* I will only add, that this hope needed not the Anti-Slavery Society, for in this hope colonizationism " lives, moves, and has its being."

With due respect,

Yours, &c.

LETTER XIV.

Sir,

Your next chapter, is on " the *Safety* of Immediate Emanci·
pation," which you admit that " many may conscientiously
doubt." Whether such will have their doubts removed by any
thing you have written, is even more than doubtful, for in no
part of your volume do you exhibit more deplorable evidence of
" want of information," nor do you elsewhere furnish greater
examples of illogical and sophistical reasoning.

In all the *five* cases of " immediate emancipation," to which
you appeal in proof of its safety, there was no semblance of immediateism in the case, except in the single instance of
Mexico.* In Chili, Buenos Ayres, Colombia, and New-York
every body knows that abolition was *gradually* effected, and
yet they are all cited as instances of " sudden abolition," and
as " facts" supporting your " theory." Indeed you seem to feel

---

* In this reference to Mexico, Mr. Jay is convicted of a most calam
itous " want of information," or rather inaccuracy of information
He says that " the government of Mexico granted *instantaneous* and
unconditional emancipation to every slave," and on page 190 he tells
us that " Mexico abolished slavery, *without compensating the masters.*
He will excuse me for " dispelling his ignorance" in relation to
Mexico, as he proposes kindly to do for others, in the case of St. Domingo.

The facts of the case in Mexico, are exactly the reverse, and as his
reference to it is unfortunate, so also his reasoning on it is fallacious.
The slaves in Mexico were " all declared free at once, but were con·
sidered *in debt to their former masters, to the amount of the money for
which they might have been sold before emancipation*, and they wer·
obliged to remain on the plantations and labour as formerly, till the·
had paid that debt by their labour ; and a police system was establish·
ed to enforce this regulation. The amount of it was, that the law
secured to them the privilege of buying their freedom, which the·
generally accomplished in the course of TWELVE YEARS !"

If this is what Mr. Jay calls " instantaneous and unconditiona
emancipation," we should regard it only as another " *triumph of gradualism.*"

hat your materials for making this chapter were insufficient, and you therefore abruptly terminate it by a reference to the ' Scenes in St. Domingo," and promise in the next chapter to " dispel the *ignorance*" which you say extensively prevails on this subject, and confirm the truth of the safety of immediate emancipation. I say nothing of the modest insinuation that the history of St. Domingo, is a subject on which so " extensive ignorance prevails," that you are called upon and prepared to " dispel" it.

I suppose that you will not maintain this charge of ignorance against the venerable Clarkson, but will admit that he knew nearly as much in relation to emancipation in St. Domingo as yourself. Let me direct your attention to his testimony then, merely premising that he contended for a "*preparatory school*" which fitted the slaves " *by degrees* for making a good use of their liberty." And adds his testimony in favour of gradual emancipation, and utterly disclaims the project of immediate abolition in the following words.

"I never stated that our West Indian slaves were to be emancipated *suddenly*, but BY DEGREES. I always, *on the other hand*, took it for granted, that they were to have a *preparatory school* also." Nor does that venerable philanthropist and friend of the African race, refer to a single example to show the desirableness of " *sudden*" emancipation.

The following paragraph is from an excellent sermon by the Rev. Joseph Tracy, and the extracts are made from Mr. Clarkson's thoughts.

"In February, 1794, the directory passed a decree for the abolition of slavery in the colonies. Now notice the *conditions* of this emancipation. 1. ' The labourers were *obliged* to hire themselves to their masters, for not less than a year; at the end of which, but not before, they might quit the service and engage with others.' 2. ' They were to receive a third part of the produce of the estate, as a recompense for their labour.' 3. After Toussaint, a negro, came into power, about the end of 1796, he 'took away from every master the use of the whip, and of the chain, and of every other instrument of correciion, either by himself or his own order: he took away, in fact, all power of arbitrary punishment.' He increased the term of service from one year to five years, and reduced the compensation from one third to one fourth of the produce. He 'succeeded in making the black labourers return to the plantations, there to resume the drudgery of cultivation.' Notice the words *return* and *resume*. It appears, then, that the negroes, *after* what is called their emancipation, were *obliged* to work for the planters, *at first* without the privilege of choosing their masters, and *always* at a price fixed by others, and till the time of Toussaint, were liable to be driven to their labours by the whip or some 'other instrument of punishment,' applied at the discretion oɪ their employers ; and the result was such, that Toussaint was thought to do wonders, when he made them *return* to the plantations and *resume* their 'drudgery.' Does this prove 'the safety, practicability, and expediency of *immediate* emancipa tion ?' And do those among us, who advocate immediate eman cipation, mean that our slaves should immediately be put intc the condition just described?"

Here then it is demonstrated, that if all you say in relation to the scenes of St. Domingo, be admitted, so far from being, as you pretend, a "glorious demonstration of the *perfect safety* ot' *immediate* and *unconditional* emancipation," it furnishes irrefragable evidence against your doctrine, since, in this case, the abolition was both " *gradual* and *conditional.*"

Mr. Tracy proceeds:—

"Another case mentioned by Clarkson is that of the slaves in Colombia, South America, where a decree was passed, July 19, 1821, giving freedom to all slaves who had served in the armies of the republic, and providing that all born after the date of the decree should be free at the age of eighteen. This is gradual emancipation, again, on the same principle adopted in New York.

"The last case mentioned by Clarkson, is that of the Hon. Joshua Steele, of Barbadoes, of which he says, 'It took him six years to bring his negroes to the state of vassalage described, or to that state from whence he was sure that they might be transferred without danger, in no distant time, to the rank o. free men, if it should be thought desirable.' 'Immediate abo lition,' truly !

" So far, then, not a single instance is found, of the 'imme diate emancipation' of all the slaves of any country. In every instance brought forward by the advocates of that doctrine, they were emancipated, not 'suddenly,' but by 'degrees,' as Mr Clarkson maintains they ought to be. Even now, in England, a strong effort has been made to procure 'immediate emancipa-'on.' They must all be made free in a moment; but according to the bill which the friends of that measure have carried through Parliament, that *moment* is to be several years long. Why is this? Emancipation, we are told, ought not to be gradual. The demands of justice require that it be done '*instanter.*' Accordingly, a bill is brought in, which enacts, that it shall be done in twelve years. If gentlemen mean, emancipation in twelve years, why do they not say so? Why agitate the country, by calling it 'immediate?' And why compel us to understand them literally, by using arguments, which, if they proved any thing, would prove that it ought to be, strictly, immediate?

"Indeed, it does not seem, that any body seriously means to practice on the theory of immediate emancipation. It is used merely for the sake of *producing excitement.* The Jacobinical argument is the shortest, and most exciting to shallow thinkers, of any yet invented. It proves, however, if it proves any thing, that slaves ought to be emancipated,—as Clarkson says they *ought not,*—'suddenly,' and without any 'preparatory school.' And it proves, with equal force, that all slaves, and all women, and all children, should at once take part, equally with others, in the civil government of the country. And then it proves, that if any of them choose not to obey the laws of that government, they have an 'unalienable right' to set them at defiance."

Your next chapter is on the subject of emancipation in the British West Indies, which, although called by your fellow labourer, Garrison, nothing but a "triumph of gradualism;" yet you refer to it, as in the former cases, to prove that "the emancipation most conducive to the safety and happiness of the whites, is immediate and unconditional," and declare, that as the "apprenticeship system" was adopted "contrary to their *advice,* and is inconsistent with the doctrines they *profess,*" they are not responsible for its consequences. It is lamentable, indeed, that the "*responsibility*" of abolitionists could not have been secured for the " safety" of the colonies, by the British government, when this vast advantage might have been acquired by taking their *advice* and adopting the doctrines they *profess!* I suppose, however, this important measure was incidentally overlooked by the British government, in their efforts to conciliate the West India proprietors, and hence the error was committed, of making the emancipation *gradual*, instead of *immediate*, and the right of " property," unfortunately acknowledged, by the provision for " compensation to the owners."

But you next attempt to urge objections against *gradual* abolition, " on the ground of mere political expediency," alleging that while this process was unexceptionable in New York, yet it would be dangerous in South Carolina, " for the weight of the objections to gradual emancipation," you tell us, is "proportioned to the number of slaves to be emancipated," compared with the white population. But you lose sight of the reasons which influenced John Jay, that profound and sagacious statesman, to labour in behalf of *gradual* abolition in New York,* where there were so few slaves, and which prevented him, even under *these circumstances*, from ever dreaming of *immediate* abolition. And if those reasons had any weight in New York, by what process of sophistry can you deceive yourself into the belief, that it would be " safe and happy" to effect " *instant abolition*" in South Carolina.

You significantly ask "what would become of the 10,000 slaves," if so many were annually liberated in that state, on this plan of gradual abolition? And I ask you in turn, what would become of forty times that number, if South Carolina were to issue the decree of immediate and unconditional emancipation? As you call the former an " extravagant supposition," " visionary in the extreme," by what epithet would you designate the latter? And yet you say, that gradual emancipation is so dan-

---

* It is a remarkable fact, that the bill for immediately abolishing slavery in the state of New York, and which was passed in 1817, was introduced into the legislature by President Duer, the respected president of the New York City Colonization Society.

gerous, that the only alternative is "*immediate emancipation or continued slavery.*" You forget the "colonization delusion," or have probably persuaded yourself, that with the publication of your book, the epitaph is written for that powerful institution, whose funeral orgies were celebrated at the first anniversary of the American Anti-slavery Society, in May last. Know, then, that there is another and a better alternative, and learn from the Book of Revelation, that in the Divine economy for every moral evil in the universe, there is an adequate remedy. And believe me, when I assure you, that it is the deliberate conviction of many of the most exalted intellects, and the most benevolent hearts in this nation, that the American Colonization Society is destined in the order of Divine Providence to triumph over every obstacle, and prove itself the dispenser of liberty and religion, in interminable blessing upon two worlds.

The dangers of slavery on which you expatiate in your last chapter, are fully appreciated by the Colonization Society, and this is a consideration among others, which has been urged by its friends from the beginning, in favour of this institution; while at the same time, it is one, which ought to palsy the tongue and wither the hand that should be employed to magnify or increase those dangers. In my next letter, I shall briefly examine this subject.

With due respect,
Yours,

LETTER XV.

Sir,

In this concluding letter I invite your attention to the subject of "foreign interference" with the subject of American slavery ; the propriety of which, you not only justify, but advocate, since you attribute the resistance felt and expressed, against British emissaries, to national and criminal "*pride !*"

Indeed, this defence of " foreign interference," was necessary on your part, as the avowed champion of the American Anti-Slavery Society, because of the position that institution now occupies before the American community. Already have two British agents been employed for the purpose of enlightening our citizens in relation to their duty to the coloured population of our country. The society cannot enlist agents in sufficient numbers, or of sufficient popularity, in our own country, and therefore, they import British agitators, in the capacity of anti-slavery lecturers. The most distinguished of these, is George Thompson, sometimes called Rev., and at others, Esq. ; who is peregrinating through the northern and eastern states, where there are no slaves, and to whom allusion has been made in a former letter. Your defence of " foreign interference," may probably be regarded as a kind of apology for this feature in the anti-slavery tactics, though all this will fail in protecting him from the scorn and indignation of every American, whose spirit of patriotism is not extinguished by the *esprit du corps*, which is characteristic of abolitionism.

But it seems, you would not only have your countrymen listen to him and other foreign demagogues, but you attempt to intimidate the slaveholders, by foreign opinions and British threats. And can you deceive yourself by the vain hope, that you can frighten Americans by the anathemas of foreigners, or bully them into political orthodoxy by British doctrines ? Why else did you introduce the " coarse invective" of that great agitator Daniel O'Connell, together with other British "arguments addressed to the understandings and consciences of American slaveholders ?" I confess, I blush for your degeneracy from the principles of your illustrious sire, while I make the following extracts from your book.

"Mr. Buckingham, member of parliament, lately asserted at a public meeting :—

" The greater proportion of the *people of England* DEMAND not merely emancipation, but the immediate emancipation of the slaves, *in whatever quarter of the world they may be found.*"

When England becomes mistress of the world, her "people" may *demand* what they please ; but she and they know America too well, to press this *demand* in this "quarter of the world !" There is too much of the spirit of '76 and of old John Jay yet lingering among our countrymen, to withhold the expression of their indignation, at the insult which the repetition of such language conveys.

But again I quote from your book another British argument.

"Daniel O'Connell, shortly before the abolition of slavery in the British dominions, declared in public :—

" The West Indies will be obliged to grant emancipation, and then *we will turn to America*, and REQUIRE emancipation !"

Prodigious ! And the American Anti-Slavery Society and its British agent, George Thompson, I suppose, are the chosen instrumentality of Daniel O'Connell, now that he " turns to America, and *requires* emancipation." You, sir, and he, and they, will *require* it in vain. Nay, by this very attitude and union with such agitators, you close the southern ear, and harden the southern heart, and blast the hopes of all who labour and pray for emancipation. Southern hearts and southern consciences are accessible to moral suasion ; but while southern Americans yield much to courtesy, they will submit nothing to intimidation. Nor will they permit interference or dictation from any of the other states of this confederacy, as the history of this nation has amply shown. Much less will they suffer foreigners to meddle with their vested rights, or Englisnmen to *demand or require* any thing at their hands. Having aided during our revolutionary struggle in breaking the British yoke, their necks will never bend to receive another. I marvel that you did not know them better than to quote such instances of the consummate arrogance of John Bull, in reading a homily on emancipation to American slaveholders.

But the following disgraceful sentiment of O'Connell, you introduce in this connexion, to teach Americans the nature of British "public opinion," against which you say, "our fleets and armies will be of no avail." And you even threaten the citizens of the south that "when they visit Europe they will not be admitted to the usual courtesies of social intercourse," because of the "temper of the British populace." But let us attend to your extract and authority.

"When an AMERICAN comes into society," said Daniel O'Connell, in a numerous assembly, "he will be asked, 'Are you one of the THIEVES! or are you an honest man? *If you are an honest* man, then you have given liberty to your slaves; if you are among the THIEVES, the sooner you take the *outside of the house* the better!'"

And here let me ask you, sir, whether this is one of the "arguments" of the Anti-Slavery Society, "addressed to the understanding and conscience of slaveholders to *persuade* them to emancipate!" Is this one of the means you are using to promote abolition? Is this the gospel which you are bound to "GO! and preach to every creature?" And can you persuade yourself, that a book containing such language, and exhibiting such a spirit, comports with the character of an American, citizen, much less an American Christian? such as is the Hon. William Jay?

I am shocked at the state of mind and feeling to which abolitionism has reduced you, sir, when you here record, page 201, your expectation, and evidently your desire, that this temper, which denominates Americans THIEVES, in the coarse invective of O'Connell, "will, in time, become the *temper of all Europe,* and indeed, of *all the world!*" Pardon me when I say, that if your prediction be ever fulfilled, and the temper of Daniel O'Connell be the temper of all Europe and of all the world, then will civilization degenerate into barbarism, and Christianity will have left the earth for a higher, holier abode.

If this is to be, as you tell us, the result of "the progress of liberal principles," in the name of all that is rational in common sense, in the name of all that is sacred in religion, I ask, whence are those principles derived? Daniel O'Connell, the champion of "liberal principles" forsooth? And in the progress of these liberal principles "when an *American* comes into society in England," he is to be asked, "are you one of the *thieves?*" This may be the design and tendency of the anti-slavery "principles," but their claim to being "liberal" would be truly questionable. And if such be the effect of the temper of the British populace, from such "liberal principles," all good men should fervently and unitedly pray, "Good Lord deliver us."

It is painful to discover that as you proceed toward the conclusion of your "Inquiry," your intemperate spirit of declamation in no measure declines. Hence you introduce in your last chapter the couplet of "slaveholders and *colonizationists,*" who, you say, "*delight* to expatiate on the danger of immediate emancipation, and to *represent* its advocates as *reckless incendiaries* ready to *deluge the country in blood!*" In no part of your own book do you furnish a single instance in which the advocates of immediate emancipation are so *represented*, much less do you attempt any proof that colonizationists *delight* in such representations. When the rash and intemperate publications of the party, and the violent calumnies of the entire south, are rebuked by showing their pernicious tendency, and when the dangers which are justly apprehended from such measures are referred to by colonizationists, it is done with pain and mortification, instead of "*delight,*" as your own quotations from colonizationists amply demonstrate.

The dangers to be apprehended from the continuance, the increase, and perpetuity of slavery in the United States, is a theme on which the Colonization Society has dwelt with far more emphasis and effect, than is discoverable in all the writings of abolitionists, your own included. To be sure, the spirit, temper, and object for which they refer to these dangers, is vastly different from yours, and hence they have done so in strong language, without doing mischief or giving offence ; and in this respect there is a wide difference. You refer to them, accompanying your reference with bitter invective, and for the purpose of *intimidating* the south to immediate and unconditional emancipation; while colonizationists allude to them with expressions of sympathy and kindness, and with the design of convincing masters of the policy and duty of gradual abolition, and preparation for ultimate and entire abolition. In all the writings of colonizationists no attempt is made to frighten slaveholders by such language as you employ on page 198, when you say as an argument in favour of immediate abolition,

"Before they refuse to retreat from the VOLCANO on which they are *standing*, let them *look* into the *terrific crater* which *yawns beneath them !*"

The following paragraph of your book claims a specific notice, as it affords a specimen of the sophistry by which your self-complacency is inspired, and others may be and doubtless are seduced from their principles, and misled into the purest fanaticism.

" But it is demanded, with an *air of supercilious triumph,* what have *northern* men to do with slavery, and what right have they to interfere with the domestic institutions of the south ?   And is this question addressed to the followers of Him who commanded his disciples to ' go into all the world and preach the gospel to every creature ?' As well might it be asked of the Christians of America, what have they to do with the religion of Brahma; what right have they to interfere to rescue the widow from the burning pile, or the devotee from the wheels of Juggernaut ?   Christians are no less bound by the injunction to ' do good unto all men,' to endeavour by lawful means to break the fetters of the slave, than to deliver the victim of Pagan superstition."

So, then, the interference with the subject of slavery, as sanctioned by their laws, so justly complained of in the south, is here attempted to be justified by an appeal to the Scriptures. And a comparison is profanely instituted between the inculcation of anti-slavery doctrines and the preaching of the gospel of Christ ; while the civil, political, and domestic institutions of a large portion of the United States, are compared to the superstitions of paganism. But where is the warrant from

Scripture for preaching against paganism *only* in Christian countries, and creating hostility towards pagan superstition in those
countries where paganism *is not ;* and what widow would be
rescued from the funeral pile by preaching in China instead of
Hindostan; and what victim would be snatched from the wheels
of Juggernaut by *anti-pagan* lectures delivered in New-York?
And if "immediate abolitionism" be the gospel personified,
as you seem to imagine, why do you not fulfil the commandment you unfortunately quote, "GO ye into all the world, and
preach the gospel to every creature!" It is an idle conceit to
suppose that *standing still* in the north, and preaching *this*
gospel, is to GO into the south; and if the doctrines of anti-
slavery be, as you pretend, the very essence of the gospel, its
preachers are bound to GO into all the world.* It is no excuse
to say they should be persecuted, for He who commands has
said, " I send you as lambs among wolves ;" and still He says
GO, and they who hear and obey can in no wise be released
from the obligation. But the truth is, that no one in the ranks
of anti-slavery, whatever he may profess, believes that it is the
gospel, else he would go and preach where *slavery is.* Indeed
you admit it, for you say, "the obligation is *imperative,* and
they who duly respect its authority will not be *deterred* by
violence or *denunciation* from obeying its monitions." That
no one among the hosts of abolitionism act upon this "*imperative obligation,*" is a practical proof that they are all skeptics
or unbelievers in their profession of *this* gospel, else some one
would say, "neither count I my life dear to me," "I am ready
to go to prison or to death, for a testimony to the truth."

---

* Mr. Jay seems to deceive himself into the belief that he fully dis-
charges the "imperative obligation" of "GOING into all the world to
preach" this gospel, by quietly *sitting in his study* in Bedford, West
Chester County, New-York, and writing an *anti-slavery book. Such*
"missionaries" are numerous in the anti-slavery ranks, and if the
victims of pagan superstition and idolatry in heathen lands can be
rescued by such "missionary labours," Drs. Coke, Carey, and Mor-
rison, have spent their lives in vain, and Gutzlaff might be forthwith
recalled from China, and the salvation of the heathen be accomplished
by *labours,* dispensed without danger, or sacrifice of means or of life.
Alas! such preaching against paganism would accomplish all that is
desirable, only as soon as Mr. Jay's book, and preaching *his* gospel in
the *north,* will effect the abolition of slavery in the *south.*

That such is the spirit and practice of true gospel ministers, you will not question, I am sure. The missionary character of the church of Christ abounds in examples of self-sacrifice to which the gospel constrains its ambassadors, and faith is mighty to compel to the discharge of this "imperative obligation." Indeed the entire south is now a missionary field, and the millions of slaves, for whose temporal bondage your commisseration is declared, and for the "instant emancipation" of whose bodies you so zealously contend, are included in that world for whom Christ died, and to whom he directed his gospel ministers to GO. But while anti-slavery preachers, who have truly "another gospel," are deterred from going by apprehensions of "violence and denunciation," the true missionaries of the cross, taking their lives in their hands, do *go*, and will continue to *go*, preaching deliverance to the captives, and the "opening of the prison doors to them that are bound." And if they cannot deliver their bodies from involuntary servitude, they will labour and pray for their spiritual emancipation, that they may enjoy the liberty of the gospel, and become "free men and women in Christ Jesus." The Missionary Society of the Methodist Episcopal Church alone, has *scores of missionaries*, living and dying in this work of preaching the gospel, *exclusively to the slaves*, and hundreds of the ministers of that church are labouring in those sections of our country where a large proportion of their congregations are *slaves*. And this church has no less than *seventy thousand church members*, who maintain the Christian character by their walk and conversation, among *these slaves*, who, you say, are "compelled to live without God, and die without hope ;" and thus, by one fell swoop, you doom them all, and their inhuman masters, to *endless perdition !* Besides these, there are very many ministers of other denominations, who are spending their lives in this work of preaching the gospel to the slaves. You have probably seen the "Journal of a Missionary to the Negroes in the State of Georgia," which has been published in the New-York Observer, and other religious papers. That missionary is himself a slaveholder. He is devoting his time, his wealth, his life, to the work of promoting among the slaves, that godliness which is "profitable to all things having the promise of this life, and that which is to come." There are other slaveholders, men of wealth, of talent, of learning, who have consecrated themselves to this work ; and planters are numerous, who welcome these men to their plantations, and assemble their slaves, to be instructed by them, and to unite with them in the worship of God. Extensive associations of planters are formed, for the purpose of giving system and energy to these operations.

" The late revivals of religion in the southern states have produced a mighty influence in this direction ; an influence of which, at the south, few are ignorant, and the existence of which none dispute. You may learn the fact from their political newspapers even. Men there are beginning to feel extensively, that the doctrine of our text is true ; that God 'hath made of one blood all nations of men,—that they should seek the Lord ;'—that he has given them one common nature, and one common gospel, to which all ought to have access. They are beginning, more and more, to act on this principle ; and it will have the same effect which it had when Paul preached it, and men embraced, it at Athens and at Rome ;—it will abolish slavery. If slave laws remain as they are, it will render them inoperative, for it will remove all occasion for the use of them. If laws need to be altered, it will alter them. It will prove the wisdom of God, and the power of God unto salvation, not only to the individuals who receive it, but to the community which it pervades."*

The following appropriate extract, from the sermon to which allusion has just been made, is so much better expressed than I can hope to do it, that I here avail myself of it as worthy of the excellent and benevolent author, to whose head and heart these sentiments do equal honour.

" If it be conceded, that slaves are *not* a part of those for whom Christ died, and do *not* need to be saved as we do 'by the foolishness of preaching,' then it will be impossible to prove that they have any more rights than any other animals for which Christ did not die, or that they have any more claim to any emancipation at all, either immediate or remote, than

---

* Rev. Mr. Tracy's Sermon.

our oxen and horses have. But, if they are a part of the human race; if the Saviour did indeed shed his blood for them as well as for us; if faith in that gospel of his grace, which they cannot 'believe' till they 'hear' it, be necessary to save them from eternal perdition, and capable of raising them to perfect and endless felicity; and if, like other men, they are not immortal, but are actually dying—going into the eternal world, whether prepared or not, every day and every hour; then certainly it becomes us to lose no time in sending them the gospel. They need the gospel, more than all things else; as much more, as hell is worse than their present condition, as heaven is better than the condition of a free negro in the United States, and as eternity is longer than human life. Give them, then, the gospel. Let those who can, encourage, and aid, and sustain the preachers. Let those who can, whether from the pulpit, the press, or in any other way, urge upon planters the duty of having the gospel preached to them. And let those who can do nothing else, if any such there be, pray that it may be preached to them. Let Christians, at the north and at the south, give to this object, the conversion of the slaves to Christ, the prominence of which it is worthy; let them think of it, and pray for it, and, as they can find opportunity, labour for it, in proportion to its worth, and as the Spirit of Christ dictates, and they will be converted; their masters will labour for their conversion, and for their complete sanctification, and God will bless their labours, and the work will be done.

" Now we ask, is it wise, is it kind, is it Christian, to neglect this great object, and to expend all our strength, and all our zeal, and endeavour to make all others expend all their strength and their zeal, on an object which, however important, is infinitely less important to the negroes than this? Or, if attention to this object be not wholly omitted, is it wise, or kind, or Christian, to draw off the attention of the friends of the negroes from it, by making any other object more prominent? Would Paul have done it? Would Christ? Should you do it, and do it successfully; and should the result be, that all the slaves in the nation should be emancipated, and that thousands should die in their sins, who, but for the direction which you gave to the public mind, might have been saved,—do you think you should rejoice in it, when standing with them before the judgment seat of Christ?

"If you say, your object is to bring the whites to repentance for the sin of suffering them to remain in civil bondage; I ask, is it right to do this, by withdrawing their minds from the still greater sin, of suffering them to remain in bondage to Satan?

"If it be said, that we must procure their release from civil bondage, before the gospel can be successfully preached to them; what is this, but to disparage the gospel of Christ, as an insufficient remedy for the miseries of the human race,—as not adapted to the wants of men, in some of the circumstances in which they may be placed?

"Is it not plain that men who take such a course, are not as they should be;—that they have given to the temporal an ascendency over the spiritual in their own minds, for which they ought to be penitent? And when we remember that the right course would bring to those now in slavery, inevitably, safely, and pleasantly to all concerned, all the *temporal* benefits which these men are endeavouring in vain to secure to them by the wrong course—is not the imperfection of their wisdom as manifest as the imperfection of their piety?—I mean exactly what I say. I have no doubt that many of them possess both wisdom and piety; but both are imperfect, and here is a striking instance of their imperfection."

Suffer me, sir, affectionately to commend the foregoing pious sentiments to your calm and prayerful reflections. And after you shall "pause, reflect, and pray," ask yourself whether in your denunciations against slaveholding, your plea in behalf of immediate abolition, and your crusade against *colonization,* you do not neglect the "weightier matters of the law;" and whether your zeal has not got the better of your discretion, and blinded your moral vision to the "more excellent way." You and I are hastening to the judgment of the great day, with the millions of the bond and free, when nought but "truth" will be able to stand. The question between us is not, therefore, whether you or I be the abler controversialist, else my small measure of self-knowledge would have restrained my pen. But in the war between truth and error we are both committed for eternity, and I, therefore, regard self-sacrifice, an insignificant consideration.   The truth is greater than us both, and for the part we take in the present controversy, we are responsible here and hereafter.   Our motives are infinitely important to ourselves, in view of both worlds; and while I humbly make the profession of a sincere and conscientious conviction of duty as the predominant motive in this correspondence, I withhold not the admission of an equal purity of motive to yourself. And in the animadversions I have made upon the sentiments and tendency of your book, let me assure you that no unkind feelings to yourself have mingled in this effort to vindicate a cause which I believe to be identified with the present and future happiness of the millions who inhabit our own continent and that of Africa.   And if by inadvertence, any word or sentence shall have escaped my notice which shall wound your feelings, or indicate a want of respect to your Christian character, let it be imputed to the imperfections in my wisdom or piety, of which I am ever conscious, and for which I would fain repent.   My aim has been, however imperfectly performed, to glorify God, and overcome error with truth, nor would I consent to retain a syllable here which "dying, I would wish to blot."

With prayer that we may both be led into the right way, and that the truth may make us free, I subscribe myself,

With due respect,

Yours, &c.